Level 3 • Book 2

Themes

Earth, Moon, and Sun

Communities across Time

Storytelling

SRA Imagine It!

Level 3 Book 2

Program Authors

Carl Bereiter

Andy Biemiller

Joe Campione

Iva Carruthers

Doug Fuchs

Lynn Fuchs

Steve Graham

Karen Harris

Jan Hirshberg

Anne McKeough

Peter Pannell

Michael Pressley

Marsha Roit

Marlene Scardamalia

Marcy Stein

Gerald H. Treadway Jr.

 SRA

Columbus, OH

Acknowledgments

Grateful acknowledgment is given to the following publishers and copyright owners for permissions granted to reprint selections from their publications. All possible care has been taken to trace ownership and secure permission for each selection included. In case of any errors or omissions, the Publisher will be pleased to make suitable acknowledgments in future editions.

EARTH, MOON, AND SUN

GRANDMOTHER SPIDER BRINGS THE SUN. Text copyright © 1995 by Geri Keams. Illustrations copyright © by James Bernardin. Reprinted by permission of Northland Publishing, LLC.

Reprinted with permission of The National Geographic Society from the book SUN by Steve Tomecek. Illustrated by Carla Golembe. Text copyright © 2001 Stephen M. Tomecek. Illustrations copyright © 2001 Carla Golembe.

From EARTH by Seymour Simon. Text Copyright © 1984, 2003 by Seymour Simon. Reprinted by arrangement with Simon & Schuster Books For Young Readers, an Imprint of Simon & Schuster Children's Publishing Division. All rights reserved.

"The Universe" from ALL ABOARD by Mary Britton Miller. Copyright © 1958. Used by permission of Random House.

THE MOON SEEMS TO CHANGE by Franklyn M. Branley, illustrated by Barbara and Ed Emberley. Copyright © 1987. Used by permission of HarperCollins Publishing.

"The Sun is a Yellow-Tipped Porcupine", from WHIRLWIND IS A GHOST DANCING by Natalia Belting, copyright © 1974 by Natalia Belting. Used by permission of Dutton Children's Books, A Division of Penguin Young Readers Group, A Member of Penguin Group (USA) Inc., 345 Hudson Street, New York, NY 10014. All rights reserved.

COMMUNITIES ACROSS TIME

THE HOUSE ON MAPLE STREET by Bonnie Pryor, illustrated by Beth Peck. Copyright © 1987. Used by permission of HarperCollins Publishers.

From: ARCHAELOLGISTS: LIFE DIGGING UP ARTIFACTS by Holly Cefrey. Copyright © 2004 by the Rosen Publishing Group, Inc.

The Disappearing Island Text Copyright © 2000 by Corinne Demas. Reprinted with permission of McIntosh & Otis, Inc. Illustrations used with the permission of Ted Lewin.

WHAT EVER HAPPENED TO THE BAXTER PLACE? Story by Pat Ross. By permission of Jeanne C. Duvoisin, trustee, Roger Duvoisin, "What Ever Happened to the Baxter Place?" 1976. Text copyright (c) 1976 by Pat Ross. Illustrations copyright c 1976 by Roger Duvoisin. Reprinted by arrangement with Jeanne C. Duvoisin, trustee.

"Early Explorers" From FOOTPRINTS ON THE ROOF: POEMS ABOUT THE EARTH by Marilyn Singer and illustrated by Meilo So, copyright © 2002 by Marilyn Singer. Illustrations copyright © 2002 by Meilo So. Used by permission of Alfred A. Knopf, an imprint of Random House Children's Books, a division of Random House, Inc.

"Caring for the World". "A Sreen Prayer" by Jane Whittle (original title). Used by permission of the author.

From EARTHQUAKE! THE 1906 SAN FRANCISCO NIGHTMARE. Reprinted with permission of Bearport Publishing Co., Inc.

STORYTELLING

MCBROOM AND THE BIG WIND by Sid Fleishman. TEXT COPYRIGHT © 1967 BY SID FLEISCHMAN. Used by permission HarperCollins Publishers. Illustrations copyright © 1982 by Walter H. Lorraine. By permission of the artist.

"Ode to Family Photographs" from NEIGHBORHOOD ODES, copyright © 1992 by Gary Soto, reprinted by permission of Harcourt, Inc. this material my not be reproduced in any form or by any means without the prior written permission of the publisher.

"Aunt Sue's Stories", copyright © 1994 by The Estate of Langston Hughes from COLLECTED POEMS OF LANGSTON HUGHES by Langston Hughes. Used by permission of Alfred A. Knopf, a division of Random House Inc.

JOHNNY APPLESEED by Steven Kellogg. TEXT COPYRIGHT © 1988 BY STEVEN KELLOGG. ILLUSTRATIONS COPYRIGHT © 1988 BY STEVEN KELLOGG. Used by permission of HarperCollins Publishers.

TOMAS AND THE LIBRARY LADY Text copyright © 1997 by Pat Mora. Illustrations coyright © 1997 by Raul Colon. Published by arrangement with Random House Children's Books, a division of Random House, Inc., New York, New York. All rights reserved.

Text copyright © 1991 by Diane Hoyt-Goldsmith. Photographs copyright © 1991 by Lawrence Migdale. All rights reserved. Reprinted from PUEBLO STORYTELLER by permission of Holiday House, Inc.

STORM IN THE NIGHT by Mary Stolz. TEXT COPYRIGHT © 1988 BY MARY STOLZ, ILLUSTRATIONS COPYRIGHT © 1988 BY PAT CUMMINGS. Used by permission of HarperCollins Publishers.

SRAonline.com

 SRA

Program Authors

Carl Bereiter, Ph.D.
University of Toronto

Andy Biemiller, Ph.D.
University of Toronto

Joe Campione, Ph.D.
University of California, Berkeley

Iva Carruthers, Ph.D.
Northeastern Illinois University

Doug Fuchs, Ph.D.
Vanderbilt University

Lynn Fuchs, Ph.D.
Vanderbilt University

Steve Graham, Ed.D.
Vanderbilt University

Karen Harris, Ed.D.
Vanderbilt University

Jan Hirshberg, Ed.D.
Reading Specialist

Anne McKeough, Ph.D.
University of Toronto

Peter Pannell
Principal, Longfellow Elementary School,
Pasadena, California

Michael Pressley, Ph.D.
Michigan State University

Marsha Roit, Ed.D.
National Reading Consultant

Marlene Scardamalia, Ph.D.
University of Toronto

Marcy Stein, Ph.D.
University of Washington, Tacoma

Gerald H. Treadway Jr., Ed.D.
San Diego State University

Unit 4

Table of Contents

Earth, Moon, and Sun

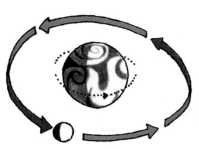

Unit 5

Table of Contents

Communities across Time

Unit 6

Table of Contents

Storytelling

Earth, Moon, and Sun

When we see a picture of our planet, Earth, it may seem small. However, when we compare it to the moon, sun, or the rest of the universe, it may seem bigger than we can imagine. Throughout time, men and women have wondered about Earth, the sun, and the moon. They asked big questions—and discovered amazing new things. Who knows how much further we can go as we study and investigate what lies beyond our planet. Let's get started!

Theme Connection

Look at the photograph. How are Earth, the moon, and the sun different? How are they similar?

BIG Idea

What can we learn when we study Earth, the moon, and the sun?

Read the article to find the meanings of these words, which are also in "Sun":

+ **devices**
+ **bursts**
+ **oval**
+ **orbit**
+ **slightly**
+ **tilted**
+ **solar system**
+ **horizon**

Vocabulary Strategy

Context Clues are hints in the text. They help you find the meanings of words. Use context clues to find the meaning of *orbit*.

Vocabulary
Warm-Up

SOHO looks at the sun around the clock. It keeps watch day after day, year after year. We know that it is not safe for us to look at the sun, even for a second. But SOHO can. SOHO is a satellite. It is one of the devices scientists use to learn about the sun.

SOHO studies all parts of the sun. It takes pictures and sends them back to Earth. Photos show that the sun is quite active. The gases and other elements that make up the sun merge and split with great force. SOHO has filmed the sun's constant bursts caused by gases.

Like Earth, SOHO moves around the sun in an oval, or egg-shaped, orbit. It keeps a steady course between Earth and the sun.

As SOHO has aged, it has become slightly worn. Some of its parts do not work as they used to. Sometimes an incorrectly tilted antenna keeps the data from being transmitted to Earth. So far, scientists have found ways to fix SOHO's problems. Soon, a new spacecraft may take its place.

SOHO has had a huge impact on our knowledge of the sun. It has helped us learn how the sun affects planets in our solar system. We can see links between weather systems on the sun and here on Earth.

When the sun slips below the horizon, we lose sight of it. However, the sun still burns and blasts, and SOHO sees it all.

GAME

Crossword Puzzle

Create a crossword puzzle with the vocabulary words. First, figure out how you will have the words overlap. Then draw empty boxes for the letters. Create separate sets of clues for words that go "Across" and words that go "Down." Give your puzzle to a classmate to complete.

Concept Vocabulary

The concept word for this lesson is **astronomy.** **Astronomy** is the study of objects in space. Throughout history, people have been curious about the planets, stars, and moons in our solar system. How do you think our understanding of astronomy has changed over time? What predictions do you have about the future of astronomy?

Genre

Expository Text is nonfiction that is written to inform, to explain, or to persuade.

Comprehension Skill

 Drawing Conclusions

As you read, look for small pieces of information that allow you to draw conclusions about a character or event in the selection. A conclusion must be supported by the text.

Sun

by **Steve Tomecek**

illustrated by Carla Golembe

Focus Questions

What role do you think the sun plays in meeting our basic needs? What role does the sun play in our solar system?

It happens every morning. You jump out of bed, and as you wipe the sleep from your eyes, you see it. The sun rises in the sky and a new day begins. Even on cloudy days the sun gives us light.

What is the sun? Why is it so bright? What makes it rise and set and move across the sky? How big is the sun, and how far is it from Earth?

To find the answers, just follow the sun.

The sun is a star. It's our star! When most people think about stars, they imagine those tiny points of light that can be seen only in the night sky.

The reason our sun seems so big and bright and other stars look like little dots is that all the other stars are much farther away. The sun is the closest star to Earth. If you could travel far into space and get close to other stars, they would look as big as our sun does.

Even though the sun is our closest star, it's still very far away from Earth. The sun is about 93 million miles from Earth. If you had to drive 93 million miles at 60 miles per hour, it would take you almost 177 years. And that's without stopping to eat a snack.

Because the sun is so far away from Earth, it doesn't look that big, but it's really gigantic. If you could measure the sun across its center, you would find that it is about 865 thousand miles across. That means that you could put 109 Earths across the face of the sun!

The sun is not made of rock, as our Earth is. It is made mostly of two hot gases called hydrogen and helium. Helium gas is what makes balloons float. It is lighter than air. Hydrogen gas is also light, and if you bring hydrogen near a fire, it explodes.

Even though it may look as if it is on fire, the sun is not burning. Explosions similar to nuclear bombs make the gases hot. The surface of the sun is more than 11 thousand degrees Fahrenheit (6 thousand degrees Celsius). If Earth were any closer to the sun, it would be too hot for us to live here.

Because the sun is so bright, you should never look right at it. Even if you are wearing sunglasses, you can hurt your eyes if you look at the sun for only a few seconds.

When scientists study the sun, they don't usually look at it directly. First, they put special filters on their telescopes, and then they use cameras to take pictures of the sun. What they have found is that the surface of the sun is constantly changing.

The sun is covered with dark and light patches. Scientists call the dark patches sunspots. They think that sunspots are a kind of giant storm. Sunspots look dark because they are cooler than the rest of the surface of the sun. The number of sunspots changes all the time.

Sometimes the sun shoots large bursts of hot gas into space. Scientists call these bursts solar flares.

Solar flares can make radios, televisions, cell phones, and other electrical devices here on Earth act weird.

Have you seen how the sun seems to move across the sky? The sun seems to rise in the east and set in the west.

Many years ago, people thought that the sun traveled around Earth. They thought that Earth was the center of everything.

Today we know that it's really Earth that is moving, not the sun. Even though we can't feel it, Earth is always spinning, just like a basketball on a player's finger. The line that Earth spins around is called an axis.

Because Earth is spinning on its axis like a big ball, sometimes you are on the side that faces the sun, and sometimes you are on the side that faces away from the sun. When you're on the side that faces the sun, the sun's light shines on you. That's daytime.

When the place you are on turns away from the sun, it gets dark. That's night. It takes Earth about 24 hours to make one complete spin. That's a day.

Besides spinning, our Earth is also moving around the sun in a slightly oval-shaped path called an orbit. It takes about 365 days—one year—for the Earth to make one trip, or orbit, around the sun. How many orbits old are you?

The axis of the Earth is tilted a bit. As our Earth orbits the sun, sometimes the place where you are is tilted toward the sun, and sometimes the place where you are is tilted away from the sun. This is why the Earth has seasons. If the Earth weren't tilted in its orbit, the season would always be the same!

During the summer, the sun appears to be high overhead in the sky. If you watch the clock, you'll see that there are more hours of daylight in the summer than in any other season. Summer is warm because the part of the Earth you are on is tilted toward the sun.

During the winter, the sun appears to be closer to the horizon. The horizon is where the sky and the ground meet. There are fewer hours of daylight and it's colder in the winter because the part of the Earth you are on is tilted away from the sun.

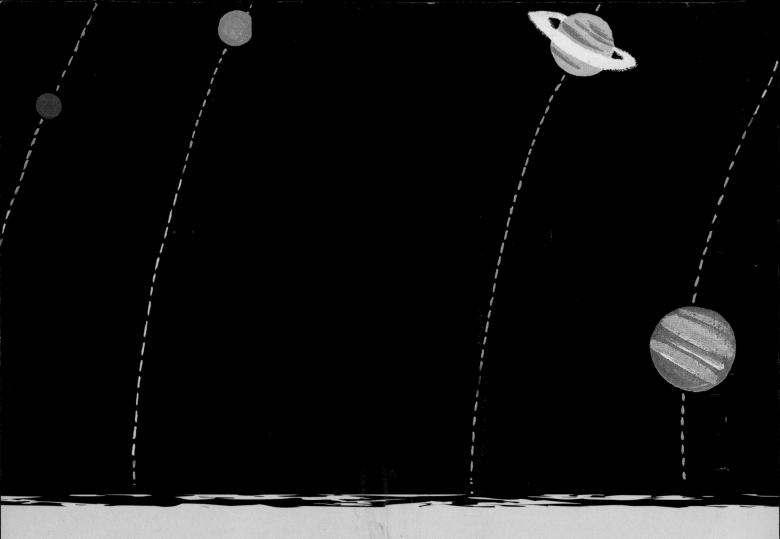

Our Earth isn't the only planet that goes around our sun. Seven other planets do too. In order out from the sun, the planets are Mercury, Venus, Earth, Mars, Jupiter, Saturn, Uranus and Neptune. Pluto used to be the ninth planet from the sun. As scientists learned more about Pluto, they decided it was different than the other planets. Pluto is now called a dwarf planet.

The sun is the center of our neighborhood in space. We call our neighborhood the solar system. Can you match each planet with its name?

Without the sun, most things would not be able to live here on Earth. Without sunlight, plants could not grow. Without plants, people and other animals would have no food.

The sun also keeps Earth warm. When sunlight hits the rocks and water on Earth's surface, some of the light is soaked up and turned into heat.

Without this heat from the sun, all of the water on Earth would freeze.

Our sun is truly special. It gives us light. It gives us life. The sun is the biggest thing in our solar system. You might even say that it's our "star" attraction.

Meet the Author

Steve Tomecek

Steve Tomecek is a geomorphologist— he studies dirt. He is known as the "Dirtmeister®" by his fans. Tomecek works hard to make science easy and fun for other people to understand. He stars in a PBS show called "Dr. Dad's Phantastic Physical Phenomena." He and his family live in New York.

Meet the Illustrator

Carla Golembe

Carla Golembe loves to paint with rich, tropical colors. In many of her paintings, there is no gravity—cats, fish, and even people may fly through the air. Golembe has illustrated children's books, greeting cards, and magazines. She teaches art and gives talks to teachers and students at elementary schools.

Earth, Moon, and Sun

Theme Connections

Within the Selection

1. What are some ways you protect yourself from the sun?

2. What is your favorite season? How is your part of Earth positioned in relation to the sun during that time of year?

Beyond the Selection

3. How is information about the sun important to all people?

4. Why is it impossible for people to visit the sun?

Write about It!

Describe how you feel when the sun does not shine for a few days.

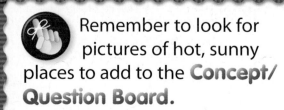

Remember to look for pictures of hot, sunny places to add to the **Concept/Question Board.**

ROY G. BIV

Have you heard of Roy G. Biv? No, this is not the name of a famous man. It is an acronym. Each letter stands for a color of the rainbow: Red, Orange, Yellow, Green, Blue, Indigo, and Violet.

We see sunlight as white light. However, white light is a blend of colors. Water refracts, or bends, light. Each of the colors that make up white light bends at a **slightly** different angle. That is how drops of rain split sunlight into the colors of the rainbow.

You do not have to wait for a rainy day to see a rainbow. You can make your own!

This is what you need:

- A smooth, clear glass jar

- A pitcher of water

- A small mirror (that will fit inside the jar)

- A sheet of white paper

- A sunny window

Genre

Explaining a Process is telling how something happens or should be carried out.

Feature

Bold Type is used for emphasis in text.

This is what you do:

1. Fill the jar with water. **Be careful when handling glass!**

2. Put the sheet of paper on a flat surface near the window.

3. Set the jar on top of the paper.

4. Put the mirror in the jar. The mirror should be tilted a bit. Make sure it reflects onto the paper.

5. Move the jar so that sunlight shines on the mirror. Look for the colors of the rainbow on the sheet of paper! If you do not see a rainbow, shift the angle of the mirror.

Think Link

1. How does water affect sunlight, or white light?

2. How does the author call attention to the safety warning in Step 1?

3. Why is it important to follow the steps of a process in the correct order?

Try It!

As you work on your investigation, think about how you can use bold type to emphasize important text.

Read the story to find the meanings of these words, which are also in "Grandmother Spider Brings the Sun":

- ✦ tight
- ✦ directions
- ✦ bushy
- ✦ ringed
- ✦ rays
- ✦ sneak
- ✦ clay
- ✦ squinty

Vocabulary Strategy

Word Structure is when parts of a word help you understand the word's meaning. Use word structure to find the meaning of *ringed.*

Vocabulary
Warm-Up

Grandpa sat cross-legged on the ground near the campfire. The wood popped and crackled in a tight circle of rocks. He waited for the children to join him.

Grandpa was a master storyteller, and the kids loved to hear his tales. They also liked their part in making up the stories. Grandpa sent the three kids into the woods. Of course, he made sure they had directions back to the camp. Each child would return with an object he or she had found.

Grandpa used the objects as props for a story. An acorn would become a rare gem. A pine branch placed just right made Grandpa's bald head suddenly bushy. A raccoon's ringed

34

tail (no one cared to think about how it was parted from its owner!) served as a king's fur collar.

Grandpa wondered what tools he would have to work with tonight. He would not have to wait long to find out. Rays from the kids' flashlights bounced near the edge of the woods.

Grandpa pretended not to notice. The kids would sneak up on him, and he did not want to spoil their surprise. Soon, they were upon him, and he let out a forced shriek.

The children laid their finds on the ground before Grandpa. There was a pinecone, clay scooped from the creek bed, and a snail shell.

Grandpa made his eyes squinty and scratched his chin. He was deep in thought. At last, he began, "Once upon a time . . ."

Charades

Use the vocabulary words to play a game of charades with classmates. Choose one of the words to act out. The first person to correctly identify the word and explain its meaning takes the next turn as actor.

Concept Vocabulary

The concept word for this lesson is **constellation.** A **constellation** is a related group of stars. Viewed together, the stars in a constellation seem to form an image. Different constellations are visible at different times of year. How is the ability to identify constellations helpful to people?

Grandmother Spider Brings the Sun

A Cherokee Story

by Geri Keams
illustrated by James Bernardin

Focus Questions

Why did people in ancient cultures make up stories about the creation of the sun? What are some other folktales about the sun you have read or heard?

A long time ago it is said that half the world had the sun, but the other side of the world was very dark. It was so dark that all the animals were always bumping into each other and getting lost.

Wolf lived on this side of the world. He was tired of everybody bumping into him and asking him for directions, for you see, Wolf could see in the nighttime.

Wolf gathered all the animals together in a big cave. He got up in front of them and crossed his arms, and he said, "I am tired of everybody bumping into me and asking me for directions."

"I have an idea," he said. "I think we should go to the other side of the world and ask them for a piece of their sun. I think if we're nice, they'll give us a piece."

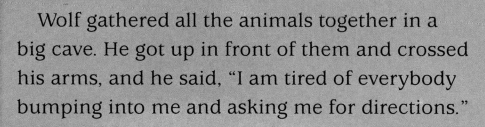

Another animal jumped up. This was Coyote, known as the trickster because he lies and cheats and steals.

Coyote said, "No, no, no, no, no! I don't think we should be so nice! If they're so nice, how come they haven't *offered* us a piece of their sun?"

The other animals nodded in agreement.

"I have a better idea," Coyote said. "I think we should sneak over there and just *steal* a piece."

"*Steal* a piece!" said Wolf. "What are you talking about, Coyote?"

"Calm down, calm down, calm down," Coyote said. "We're not going to steal a *big* piece. We'll only take a *little* piece. They'll never even miss it."

And that is what they decided to do.

Then all the animals began asking, "Who is going to go to the other side of the world? How will they get there?" Everybody had an idea, but none seemed quite right.

Then from the back of the room came a small voice. "Hey, I'll go! I'll go!"

Wolf said, "Who is that? Come down here. I can't see you."

Down to the front of the room came a little round animal with chubby cheeks. He was shy and quiet. He stood up in front of all the animals, and as he looked at all those hundreds of eyes looking back at him, he got kind of scared.

He looked out over the crowd of animals and said in his timid voice, "Hi. M-m-m-my name is Possum. I think I can go to the other side of the world. You see, I've got these long, sharp claws, and I think I can dig a tunnel. And when I go *all* the way to the other side of the world, I'll take a piece of the sun and I'll hide it in my big, bushy, tail."

And Wolf said, "Oh, a tunnel! That's the best idea yet!"

So Possum went to the big wall of dirt at the back of the cave, stuck in his sharp claws, and began to dig and dig and dig and dig, faster and faster and faster and faster. Possum disappeared inside the tunnel, and soon he had gone all the way to the other side of the world.

Now, Possum had never seen the sun, so when he popped out on the other side, the light hit his eyes, and he was blinded. His eyes got all squinty and he rubbed them with his dirty fists, saying, "Hey! I can't see!" Well, you know, Possum's eyes have been squinty and ringed with dirt ever since.

Possum struggled over to the sun, took a little piece, and put it inside his big ol' bushy tail. Then he turned around and came running back down the tunnel.

Possum ran faster and faster and faster and faster. Something started to get hot inside his tail, but Possum kept running, faster and faster.

That something got hotter, and Possum kept running faster, and he soon ran into the room where all the animals were waiting. They all saw smoke coming out of his tail, and they screamed, "Possum! Your tail! Your tail!" and threw water on him. *Whoosh! Whoosh! Whoosh!* The light was gone.

When the smoke had cleared, Wolf looked up and said, "Oh, no, Possum! Look at your tail! It's all skinny!"

And you know, Possum's tail has been this way ever since.

Wolf said, "We still don't have any sun. What are we going to do now?"

A loud voice from the back of the room said, "Send me! I'll go!"

Down to the front stormed a large bird with long black feathers all over his body, and a crown of feathers on top of his head. He held his head high and stuck his chest out as he marched importantly past the other animals. You see, this bird was a show-off. He thought he was the most beautiful bird alive.

He stood up in front of all the animal people and he said, "It's me, Big Bad Buzzard. I'll go to the other side of the world and it won't take me long at all, but I wouldn't be so dumb as to hide the light in my tail. I'm gonna hide it in my beautiful crown of feathers."

Buzzard jumped into the tunnel and soared through the darkness, and it didn't take long at all until he came out on the other side.

Buzzard took a little piece of sun, put it inside his crown of feathers, turned around, and soared back down the tunnel faster and faster and faster and faster. As he came down the tunnel, something started to get hot on top of his head.

Buzzard soared faster and faster, and something got hotter and hotter.

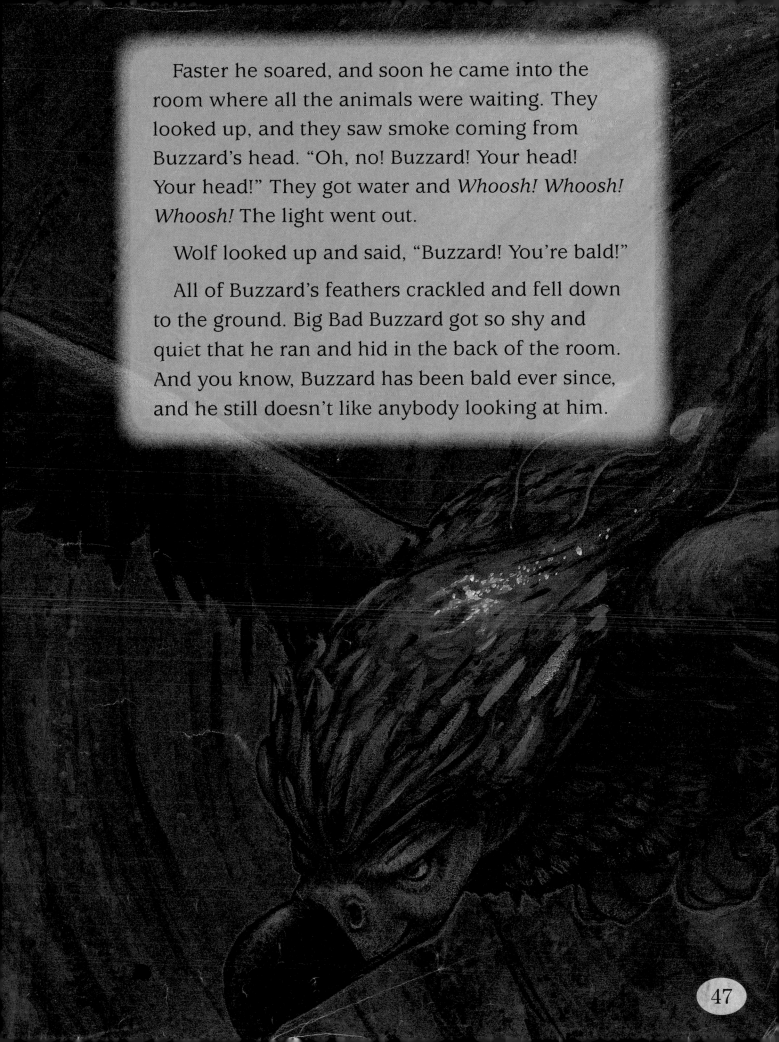

Faster he soared, and soon he came into the room where all the animals were waiting. They looked up, and they saw smoke coming from Buzzard's head. "Oh, no! Buzzard! Your head! Your head!" They got water and *Whoosh! Whoosh! Whoosh!* The light went out.

Wolf looked up and said, "Buzzard! You're bald!"

All of Buzzard's feathers crackled and fell down to the ground. Big Bad Buzzard got so shy and quiet that he ran and hid in the back of the room. And you know, Buzzard has been bald ever since, and he still doesn't like anybody looking at him.

Wolf said, "Possum's burned his tail off and now Buzzard's bald, and we still don't have any sun. What are we going to do now?"

A tiny voice from up above said, "Send me! I'll go! Hey, send me, I'll go! I'll go!"

Wolf looked all around, but he couldn't tell where the voice was coming from. "Who is that? Where are you? Come down where I can see you."

Down from the corner of the ceiling squeaked the tiny voice:

"Send me e e e e e e e e e e e e !"

And right there in front of Wolf landed a tiny spider. The spider looked up and Wolf looked down, and Wolf said, "Oh, no! Not you, Grandma! You can't go to the other side of the world. You're too old—and besides that, you're too slow!"

Well, this was Grandmother Spider. She had done many things to help the animals in her long life. She crossed her little arms and said, "I know I'm old. You don't have to tell me I'm old. But I want to help my people one more time. I need a piece of clay about so big, and you'll get me a piece, won't you, son?"

Wolf went and got Grandmother Spider a piece of clay, and she sat in the middle of the room and began to chant. Soon she had worked the clay into a little bowl.

She picked up that beautiful clay bowl and disappeared inside the tunnel. They say it took Grandma Spider a long, long, long, long time to get to the other side of the world.

The Sun Guards were out now. They knew somebody was trying to steal some of their sun, and they stood in a tight circle around it. They weren't going to let anybody through.

The Sun Guards were mean-looking monsters. They had fire coming out of their heads. They had fire coming out of their mouths: *Hissssss!* And they held their weapons, ready for a fight.

But Grandmother Spider was so tiny that they didn't even see her. She sneaked between them, went up to the sun, took a little piece, put it in her clay bowl, and sneaked back past the Sun Guards.

She came back down the tunnel *very* slowly. It took her a long, long, long, long time to get to her side of the world. And as she got closer, something happened. The light inside her bowl began to grow. The little rays stretched out of the bowl.

As she came out of the tunnel into the cave, that ball of light was growing. She could hardly even carry it.

All the animals came running to help Grandmother Spider: blind Possum and bald Buzzard, Wolf and Coyote and Bear and Deer and all the others. But that ball of light just kept getting bigger and bigger and bigger and bigger, and it got so big that the animals had to squeeze it out of the cave, and as it squeezed out into the world it bounced up into the sky: *Boingggg!*

It is said that from that day on, whenever
Grandmother Spider would spin her web,
the shape of the sun would be at the center.
And you see, Grandmother Spider spins her
web that way to this very day.

Meet the Author

Geri Keams

Geri Keams is an actress, an author, and a Navajo storyteller. She is part of the Streak-of-Black-Forest Navajo clan. As a young girl, Keams was encouraged by her grandmother to share the stories and songs of her ancestors. She loves to perform for children and has taken her children's show "Stories and Songs of My People" around the world.

Meet the Illustrator

James Bernardin

When he was young, James Bernardin and his family traveled a lot. For each trip, his parents gave him a sketchbook so that he had something fun to do. Later, Bernardin studied art in college. He has won many awards for his work. He lives in Seattle, Washington, with his wife and sons, but he still loves to travel.

Earth, Moon, and Sun

Theme Connections

Within the Selection

1. How does this story show the importance of the sun for creatures on Earth?

2. How do people get light when the sun is not shining?

Across Selections

3. How is information about the sun the same in "Grandmother Spider Brings the Sun" and "Sun"?

4. How is it different?

Beyond the Selection

5. Why is it important to learn about folklore from different cultures?

6. Why do people continue to tell folktales?

Write about It!

Make lists of animals that are active by day and by night.

Remember to write ideas for a folktale about the sun's creation to add to the **Concept/Question Board.**

Tell Me Why

Genre

Expository Text tells people something. It contains facts about real people or events.

Feature

A **diagram** is a drawing that adds to information provided in the text.

On a clear, dark night rays of light twinkle from the stars. The stars seem to dance in the sky. According to one Native American legend, that is just what is happening! The story tells of seven boys who were dancing when they should not have been.

The boys wanted to be part of a ceremony. They danced around the fire, just like their fathers. An old man told the boys to stop dancing, otherwise something bad could happen. Still, the boys did not listen.

The boys went to a secret place, where they lit their own fire. They sang as they danced in a circle. Their voices grew louder and louder as they stamped their feet.

Adults from the village followed the sounds. When they found the boys, they saw something strange. The boys' feet were not touching the ground.

With each step they took, the boys rose higher into the sky. When they reached the top of the sky, they became stars. They are still there dancing in the sky today.

This story is an example of a pourquoi tale. *Pourquoi* is a French word that means "why."

This kind of story explains why or how something came to be. Most pourquoi tales describe a part of nature.

The story of the seven star dancers is based on a real set of stars. They are known as the Pleiades. The name *Pleiades* comes from a Greek myth. Greeks have their own tale that explains the star cluster. Other cultures have still more stories about the Pleiades' origin. The tales may vary, but they all answer the same question: Why?

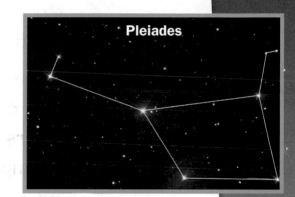

Pleiades

Think Link

1. What is the purpose of pourquoi tales?

2. How do pourquoi tales mix fact and fiction?

3. Does the diagram add to your understanding of the Pleiades?

Try It!

As you work on your investigation, think about how you can use a diagram to show information in your final presentation.

Read the article to find the meanings of these words, which are also in "The Moon Seems to Change":

- ✦ crescent moon
- ✦ sliver
- ✦ occur
- ✦ phases
- ✦ quarter moon
- ✦ new moon

Vocabulary Strategy

Context Clues are hints in the text. They help you find the meanings of words. Use context clues to find the meaning of *sliver*.

Vocabulary
Warm-Up

Have you ever seen a face looking down from the moon? In many cultures, there are myths about the "man in the moon." People have written poems and songs about him too.

The moon has high and low points. This creates shadows on the moon that we can see from Earth. Some of the dark spots on the moon seem to form eyes, a nose, and a mouth.

Look at the night sky during a full moon. This is when the moon looks very round. Can you see the shadows that make up the face of the man in the moon?

Some people see a face in a **crescent moon** too. Because a crescent moon looks like just a **sliver** of the full moon, it does not show the whole face. Instead, it shows a side view.

A crescent moon will **occur** at the start of a waxing period and the end of a waning period. Waxing is when the moon seems to get bigger; waning is when it seems to get smaller.

The man in the moon hides during some of the moon's **phases**. We cannot make out the face in a **quarter moon**—when the moon looks like a semicircle to us. This is because only half of the moon is lit by the sun.

We do not see a **new moon** at all. During this phase, the part of the moon that is lit by the sun does not face Earth. Not only is the man hiding, but so is the moon!

GAME

Writing Sentences

Use each vocabulary word in two sentences. First, use the word in a sentence that asks a question. Then use the word in a sentence that is a statement. Write your sentences on a sheet of paper.

Concept Vocabulary

The concept word for this lesson is *cycle.* A **cycle** is a series of events that happens regularly. The moon follows the same cycle as it orbits Earth. Do you think it is important for people to be aware of cycles in our solar system? Talk about your ideas with classmates.

Genre

Expository Text is nonfiction that is written to inform, to explain, or to persuade.

Comprehension Skill

 Compare and Contrast

As you read, compare and contrast familiar ideas or things with ideas or things that are unfamiliar.

Focus Questions

What different shapes and colors can the moon be? What is the relationship between the sun and the moon?

The MOON Seems to Change

by Franklyn M. Branley

illustrated by Barbara and Ed Emberley

Tonight take a look at the sky. See if the moon is there.

Full

It may be big and round. It is a full moon.

Quarter

Maybe you will see only part of it. It may be a quarter moon.

Crescent

Or it may be only a little sliver. It is called a crescent moon.

As the nights go by you can see changes in the moon. After the moon is full you see less and less of it. There are three or four nights with no moon at all. Then you see more and more of it. The moon seems to change.

It really doesn't. It seems to change because the moon goes around Earth. As it goes around, we see more of it—the moon gets bigger. It is a waxing moon. Or we see less of it—the moon gets smaller. It is a waning moon.

✵— Waxing Moon →

✵— Waning Moon →

Half of the moon is always lighted by the sun. Half is lighted and half is always in darkness. It's the same with Earth. While one half of Earth is having sunshine and daylight, the other half is getting no sunshine. It is night.

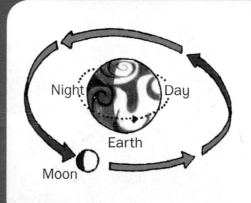

Night   Day

Earth

Moon

Sun

A day on Earth is 24 hours long.

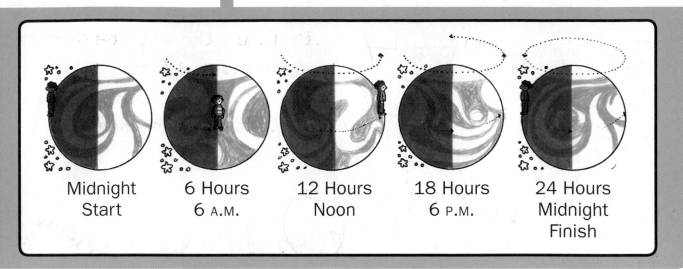

| Midnight Start | 6 Hours 6 A.M. | 12 Hours Noon | 18 Hours 6 P.M. | 24 Hours Midnight Finish |

A day on the moon is almost a month long.

It takes the moon about four weeks to go around Earth.

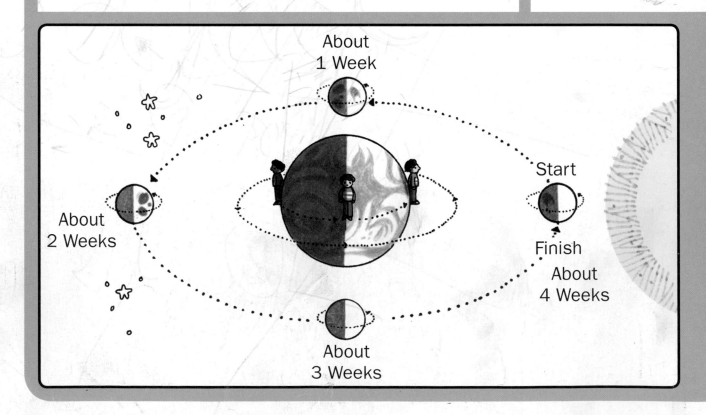

About 1 Week

About 2 Weeks

Start

Finish
About 4 Weeks

About 3 Weeks

Dark side of moon facing us so we cannot see it.

As the moon goes around Earth, it is sometimes between Earth and the sun. The dark half of the moon is facing us. We cannot see any of the lighted half. This is called new moon.

New moon not in night sky so we cannot see it.

A night or two later the moon has moved a little bit along its path around Earth. We can then see a small part of the lighted half. It is called a crescent moon. We see it just after sunset. It is in the west, where we see the sun go down. You may be able to see it before the sky is dark. Sometimes you can see it in the daytime.

Each night the moon seems to grow. The moon is waxing. We can see a bit more of the lighted half.

About a week after the moon is new, it has become a first-quarter moon. It looks like this. Sometimes you can see it in the afternoon before the sky is dark.

After another week the moon is on one side of Earth and the sun is on the other side. We can see all the lighted half of the moon. It is a full moon. We see it in the east as the sun sets in the west. We can't see it in the daytime.

Each night after it is full, we see less and less of the moon. The moon is waning. In about a week it is a quarter moon. This is third quarter. It can be seen after midnight.

After that, the moon once more becomes a crescent. Each night the crescent gets a bit thinner. We would see it later and later at night—long after we're usually asleep. A few days later we cannot see the moon at all. It is once again a new moon. About four weeks after the moon is new, we have another new moon.

Two or three nights later, the moon has become a thin crescent. Night after night the same changes occur. Keep watch on the skies and you will see the changes—new moon, crescent, first quarter, full moon, third quarter, crescent, and back to new moon. All together, the changes are called the phases of the moon.

| New | Crescent | First Quarter | Full | Third Quarter | Crescent | New |

 Phases of the Moon ✿

This is the
side of the moon
you can see
from Earth.

Until spaceships went around the moon,
we had never seen the other half of it.

The other side

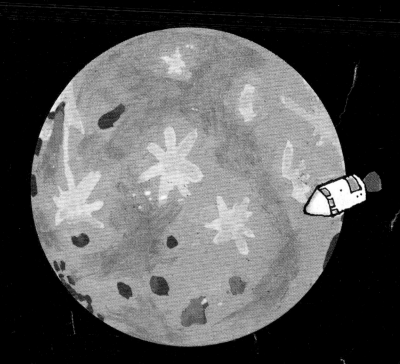

Sometimes we see a lot of the part of the moon that is turned toward us, and sometimes only a little of it. The moon grows bigger, and then gets smaller. The moon seems to change. It goes through phases because it goes around Earth.

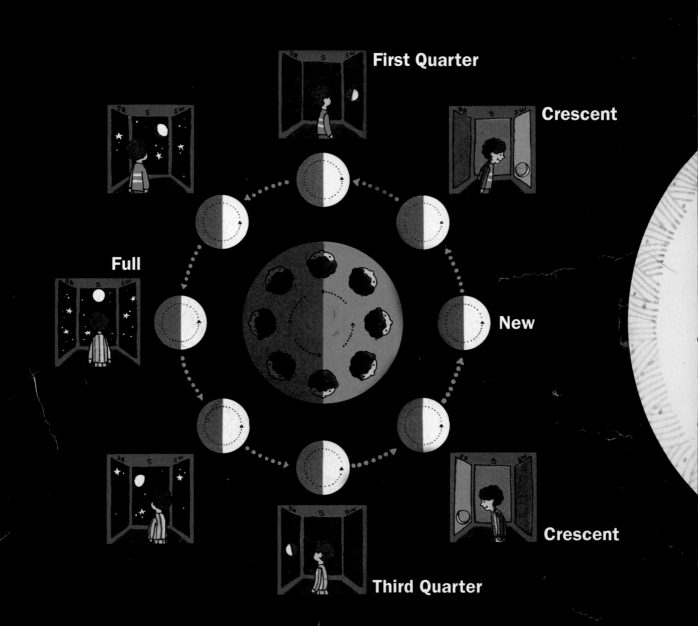

First Quarter

Crescent

Full

New

Third Quarter

Crescent

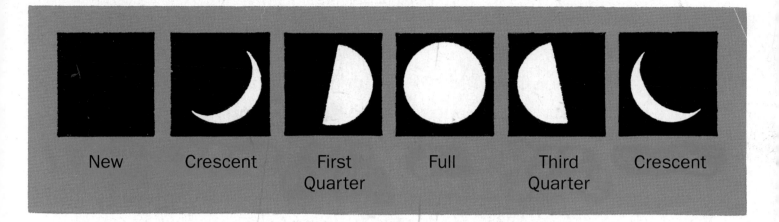

| New | Crescent | First Quarter | Full | Third Quarter | Crescent |

Which phase of the moon
can you see tonight?

Meet the Author

Franklyn M. Branley

During his career, Franklyn M. Branley wrote more than 150 children's books about science. In 1956, Branley began working as the director of the American Museum of Natural History's Hayden Planetarium. He also became an astronomer and began writing about space. He later became Chairman at the same planetarium, but retired so he could write children's books full time.

Meet the Illustrators

Barbara and Ed Emberley

Barbara and Ed Emberley have worked together on many children's books. Their children have also helped with their books. The Emberleys met at the Massachusetts School of Art in Boston, and they now live in Ipswich, Massachusetts. They run a private hand press called Bird in the Bush. The Emberleys also like to jog, ski, and sail.

Theme Connections

Within the Selection

1. How has space travel helped us learn more about the moon?

2. How is the moon necessary for life on Earth?

Across Selections

3. Think about what you read in "Sun" and "The Moon Seems to Change." How are the sun and the moon alike?

4. How are they different?

Beyond the Selection

5. How is tracking the moon's phases useful to people?

6. Where else in nature do you see a repeating pattern of change such as the moon's?

Write about It!

Compare how your neighborhood looks in daylight with how it looks in moonlight.

Remember to look for articles about the moon to add to the **Concept/ Question Board.**

All Shook Up

Use an outline to plan a report. List the main ideas and important details you want to include. Here is one student's outline for a science report.

Earthquakes and Moonquakes

I. An earthquake is caused by a break in rock beneath the earth.

   A. The break is called a *fault*.

   B. A fault is where plates (blocks of rock) meet.

   C. Plates move together and apart.

   D. Most earthquakes occur along fault lines.

II. Earthquakes create seismic waves.

   A. Waves start where rocks break or faults shift.

   B. Primary waves (P waves), sound waves traveling fast through earth, are felt as a "thud."

P waves

   C. Secondary waves (S waves), slower and more damaging, are felt as vibrations.

S waves

III. There are different types of moonquakes.
    A. Deep moonquakes happen far below the moon's surface.
    B. Shallow moonquakes are forceful and last a long time.
    C. Some moonquakes are caused when a meteor hits.
IV. Moonquakes last longer than earthquakes.
    A. Most earthquakes vibrate less than one minute.
       1. Water under the ground softens rock below Earth's surface.
       2. Soft rock absorbs the energy, and the waves do not travel too far.
    B. Moonquakes can last up to one hour.
       1. The surface of the moon is cool and dry.
       2. Cracks in the surface scatter seismic waves in many directions.

Think Link

1. In section I of the outline, why do the words *blocks of rock* appear in parentheses?

2. What types of seismic waves does the writer identify?

3. Why are the details in the last section of the outline arranged differently than in other sections?

Try It!

As you work on your investigation, think about how you can use parentheses for additional information in your outline.

Read the fable to find the meanings of these words, which are also in "Journey to the Moon":

✦ **gigantic**
✦ **astronaut**
✦ **pressure**
✦ **gravity**
✦ **orbit**
✦ **commander**

Vocabulary Strategy

Word Structure is when parts of a word help you understand the word's meaning. Use word structure to find the meaning of *commander*.

Vocabulary

Warm-Up

Mouse looks up at the full moon brightly lighting the sky. He says to his older brother, "Did you hear the news? The moon is made of green cheese!"

Mouse's brother says, "Don't believe it. That old rumor has been around for years. Besides, what would you want with that? We have all the cheese we can eat right here from the deli."

Mouse knows they have a good life in the alley. They never go hungry. However, Mouse cannot forget about the gigantic circle of cheese in the sky. He is determined to have it.

How will he do it? Can he ride a kite high into the sky? Can he sneak aboard a spaceship with an astronaut?

Hawk spies Mouse thinking over his problem. "What is up?" asks Hawk. Mouse scurries behind a trash can, hiding from his enemy. "Come here," says Hawk, "perhaps I can help you."

Mouse is so eager to get to the moon that he strikes a deal with Hawk. Mouse feels the sharp pressure of Hawk's talons on his skin. In a flash, he is flying through the air, free from the pull of Earth's gravity.

Hawk and Mouse orbit the block several times. Suddenly, they start to drop. "Higher!" yells Mouse. "Take me straight to the moon!"

"I am commander of this flight," says Hawk, "and I say it is time for a snack."

GAME

Definition Game

In a group, play a game to review the meaning of each vocabulary word. One player gives a definition, such as, "What word means leader?" The classmate who correctly names the word (*commander*) gets to choose the next definition to give to the group. Play until all of the vocabulary words have been used.

Concept Vocabulary

The concept word for this lesson is *mission*. A **mission** is a journey designed to carry out specific tasks. Astronauts as well as crew members on the ground prepare a very long time for space missions. Share your ideas about the kinds of things astronauts practice to get ready for a mission.

Genre

Expository Text is nonfiction that is written to inform, to explain, or to persuade.

Comprehension Strategy

⭐ Clarifying

As you read, make a note of sections you do not understand, and reread them to better understand what they say.

Journey to the Moon

to the Moon

by Jan Mader

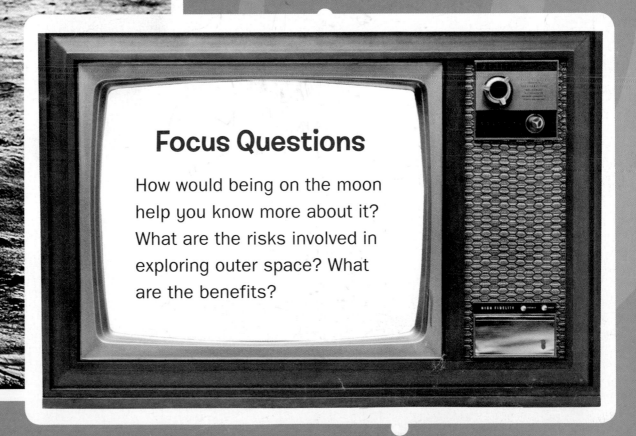

Focus Questions

How would being on the moon help you know more about it? What are the risks involved in exploring outer space? What are the benefits?

Have you ever wondered what it would be like to walk on the moon? Neil Armstrong had thought about this for a long time. On July 20, 1969, he finally found out. Armstrong was an astronaut and the commander of the *Apollo 11* rocket flight—and the first man to set foot on the moon.

Apollo 11 astronauts Armstrong, Collins, and Aldrin

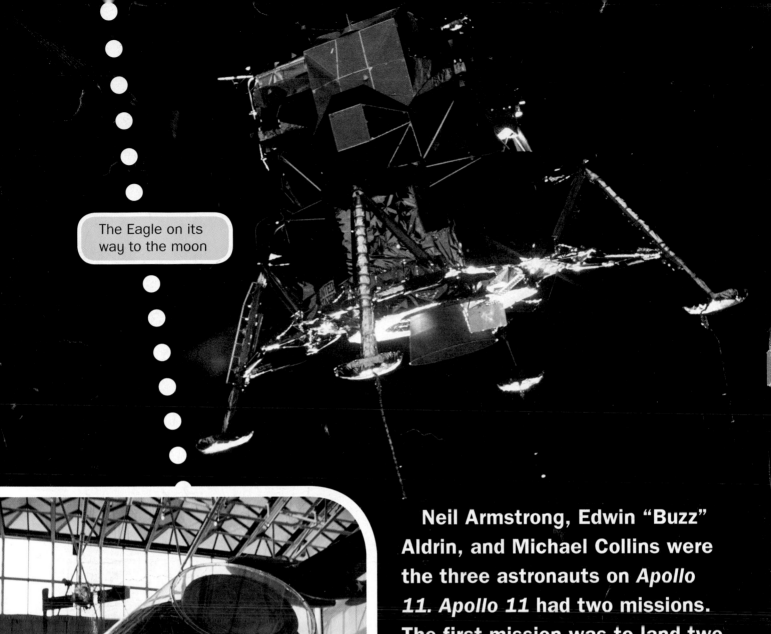

The Eagle on its way to the moon

The command module on display in Washington, D.C.

Neil Armstrong, Edwin "Buzz" Aldrin, and Michael Collins were the three astronauts on *Apollo 11. Apollo 11* had two missions. The first mission was to land two men on the moon. The second was to bring the men back to Earth safely. The spacecraft they would be using was made up of two parts. The main part, Columbia, was the command module. The second part, the Eagle, was the part that would land on the surface of the moon. It was called the lunar module. *Lunar* is a word for moon.

TV images of Armstrong stepping onto the moon

The three men blasted off from Earth on a gigantic rocket on July 16, 1969. After traveling nearly 240,000 miles, Armstrong and Aldrin crawled into the lunar module and prepared for the moon landing. Collins would orbit the moon in Columbia while his two friends visited the lunar surface. If something went wrong on the moon, he would have to return to Earth by himself.

Armstrong guided the Eagle to the moon. The landing was a success! A TV camera had been mounted to the lunar module, and over 600 million people from around the world watched as Armstrong climbed down a ladder and onto the moon. The moon's surface was dusty, and his boots left clear footprints. Finally, Armstrong spoke. "That's one small step for man, one giant leap for mankind."

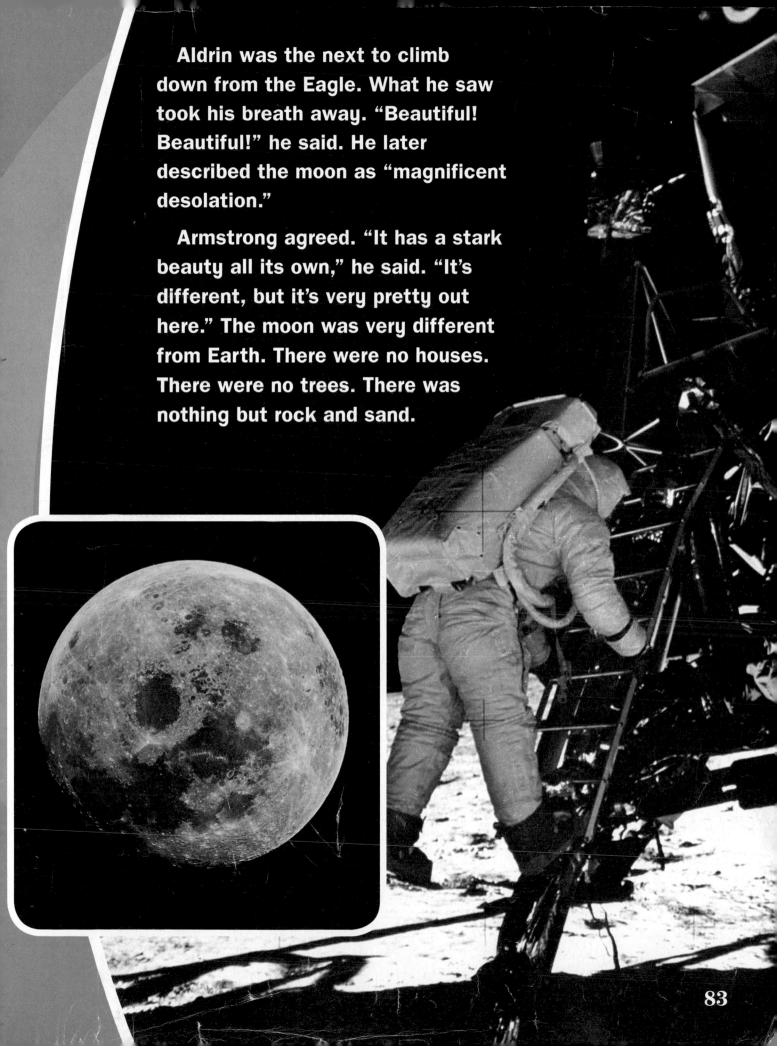

Aldrin was the next to climb down from the Eagle. What he saw took his breath away. "Beautiful! Beautiful!" he said. He later described the moon as "magnificent desolation."

Armstrong agreed. "It has a stark beauty all its own," he said. "It's different, but it's very pretty out here." The moon was very different from Earth. There were no houses. There were no trees. There was nothing but rock and sand.

The moon did seem empty and even a bit lonely. But the astronauts were very excited. They were the first humans to ever set foot on the moon. Soon they began to walk around. On Earth, people who watched their TVs saw the astronauts hopping. That's because the moon has weak gravity. It was hard for the astronauts to stand in place even though they were wearing space suits with a heavy support system on their backs. This system gave them oxygen and controlled the temperature and pressure inside their suits.

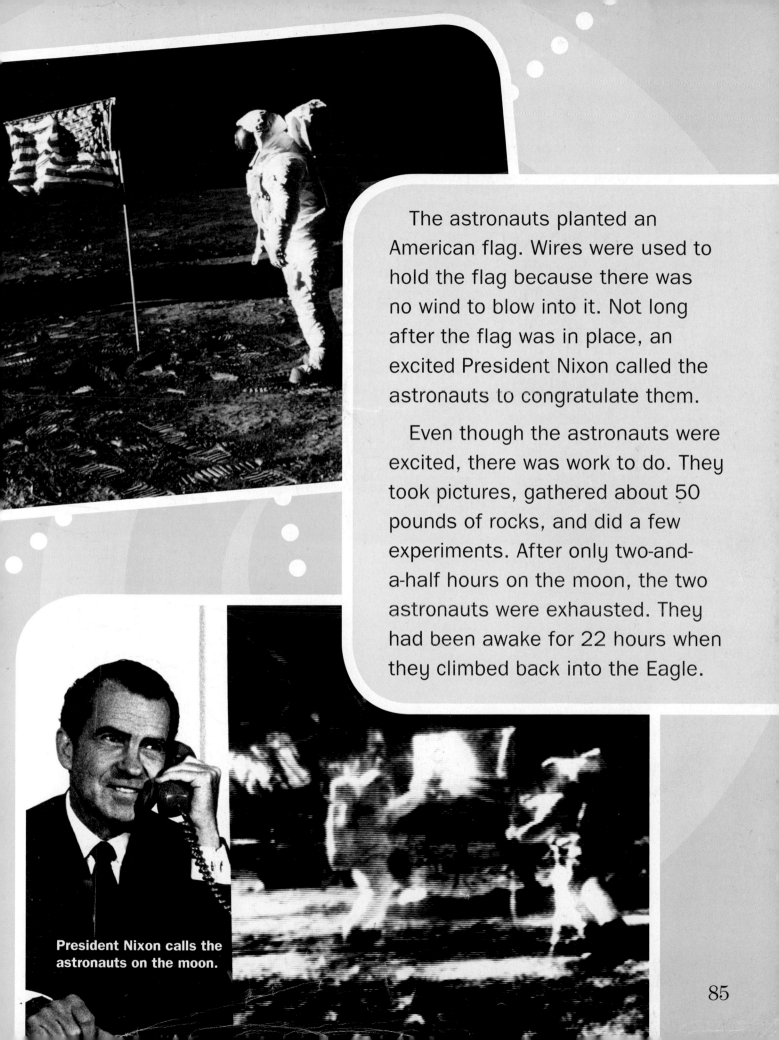

The astronauts planted an American flag. Wires were used to hold the flag because there was no wind to blow into it. Not long after the flag was in place, an excited President Nixon called the astronauts to congratulate them.

Even though the astronauts were excited, there was work to do. They took pictures, gathered about 50 pounds of rocks, and did a few experiments. After only two-and-a-half hours on the moon, the two astronauts were exhausted. They had been awake for 22 hours when they climbed back into the Eagle.

President Nixon calls the astronauts on the moon.

Neil Armstrong and Buzz Aldrin got ready to meet with the third astronaut. Michael Collins was in Columbia, nearly 70 miles above the surface of the moon. Collins had been worried about his friends on the moon. Even though Columbia passed over the landing site every two hours as it orbited the moon, Collins was too far away to see the Eagle. Also, he had no TV to watch the moon landing, and every other hour he lost radio contact with Earth as he orbited the far side of the moon.

The Eagle blasted off from the moon and docked with Columbia. Armstrong and Aldrin climbed onboard the command module. The astronauts did not need the Eagle anymore—its work was done. The Eagle fell away and crashed on the moon, and Columbia carried the astronauts back to Earth.

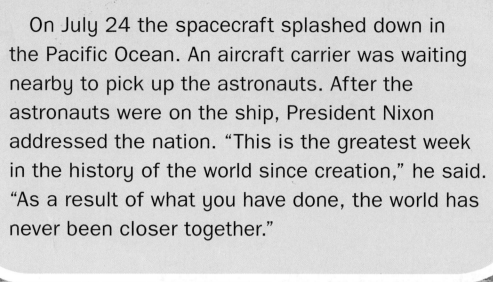

On July 24 the spacecraft splashed down in the Pacific Ocean. An aircraft carrier was waiting nearby to pick up the astronauts. After the astronauts were on the ship, President Nixon addressed the nation. "This is the greatest week in the history of the world since creation," he said. "As a result of what you have done, the world has never been closer together."

The *Apollo 11* astronauts were picked up by Navy crewmen after landing in the ocean.

As President Nixon talked, a Marine band played "The Star-Spangled Banner." But the astronauts had to watch from behind a window in a special trailer. They were in quarantine until it was certain they had carried no germs home from the moon. Later, huge parades celebrated what these heroes had accomplished.

The race to the moon had been won. Russia was the first to launch a spacecraft, and America wanted to be the first to put a man on the moon. But this was no easy task. Everything—spacecraft, space suits, booster rockets—had to be created. New technology and equipment were made as thousands of engineers worked together to make the first moon landing possible. Today many people still work to learn more. Can people live on the moon? If so, how would they do it? Only the future will tell.

Meanwhile, nothing changes on the moon. There is no air, no wind, and no rain. The footprints the two astronauts left on the moon in 1969 will be there forever. Even today they remind us of what was done in the past—and point to what can be done in the future.

Meet the Author

Jan Mader

Writing is a daily activity for Jan Mader. She writes books, magazine articles, and stories for school materials. Mader loves writing about animals, especially her horse Tango. Tango is the star of a series of books called *Tango and Tilly!* Mader has three sons and lives in Ohio with her husband Chuck and their two dogs Maddie and Kelly.

Earth, Moon, and Sun
Theme Connections

Within the Selection

1. Why do you think people from around the world were interested in the *Apollo 11* mission?

2. Would you like to travel to the moon? Explain.

Across Selections

3. How did "The Moon Seems to Change" help you understand what you read in "Journey to the Moon"?

4. What did you learn about the moon in the two selections?

Beyond the Selection

5. Why are the *Apollo 11* astronauts seen as heroes?

6. Why do countries "race" to accomplish space missions?

Write about It!

Describe an astronaut's job.

 Remember to record questions you would like to ask the *Apollo 11* astronauts to add to the **Concept/Question Board.**

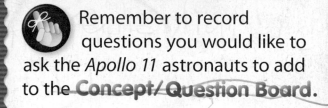

Moon Rocks to Power Earth

Genre

Expository Text tells people something. It contains facts about real issues or events.

Feature

An **apostrophe** is used to form a contraction and to show possession.

Everything is made of atoms. Atoms are particles too small to see with the naked eye. For many years, scientists have studied rocks astronauts brought back from the moon. They have discovered that some of the rocks' atoms are not found in nature.

The scientists have been able to create energy with these atoms. Scientists think we could use the energy for many things. They believe it could last for a very long time. What's more, this type of energy does not cause pollution. It is also safe to make.

If we use this energy, we will need to mine, or dig holes, into the moon. Some people think this is a bad idea. We don't know what will happen if we drill the moon for many years. It could cause changes that would affect Earth.

We need new forms of energy here on Earth. Taking rocks with special atoms from the moon may provide a solution. However, no matter what we do, we need to make sure it is safe for us—and the moon.

Think Link

1. Why do we need new forms of energy?

2. What do you think could happen if we mined the moon?

3. How is the apostrophe used in paragraph 1? How is it used in paragraphs 2 and 3?

Try It!

As you work on your investigation, remember to use apostrophes correctly in your final presentation.

Read the story to find the meanings of these words, which are also in "Earth":

- ✦ top
- ✦ scraped
- ✦ astronomers
- ✦ atmosphere
- ✦ scale
- ✦ rotation
- ✦ signs
- ✦ curve

Vocabulary Strategy

Apposition is when a word or group of words define another word in the same sentence. Use apposition to find the meaning of *scale*.

Vocabulary
Warm-Up

The lights in the gym had never seemed this bright and hot before. Today, Lin thought she might broil under them. Her pulse raced, and her head felt like a spinning top. It must have been nerves.

The school science fair was on, and Lin was waiting for the results. Each time a chair scraped against the floor, her eyes darted to the judges' table. However, they sat, talking in hushed tones.

Other junior astronomers had each done a project about space. Lin was impressed with their work. Awan's display showed how ozone forms in Earth's atmosphere. Hannah built to

scale a model of the Hubble Space Telescope, which means the size of the model represented the size of the real Hubble Space Telescope. Marie compared Earth's rotation to the other planets in the solar system. One day on Venus was like 243 Earth days!

Lin had taken a chance. She merged her love of art and science and made up a dance of the planets' revolutions around the sun. Her friends danced to show the roles of objects in the solar system. Lin thought they did a great job.

She could not tell if the judges liked it, though. Their faces showed no signs of what they were thinking. They had just thanked her and moved on.

At last, the judges stood up, and one of them came Lin's way! Lin was relieved to see the curve of a smile on his face—he was holding a blue ribbon.

GAME

Flash Cards

Make a set of flash cards with the vocabulary words. Write the word on one side and its definition on the other side. Use the flash cards to review the vocabulary words and definitions. Then ask a classmate to use the cards to quiz you.

Concept Vocabulary

The concept word for this lesson is **universe.** The **universe** is everything that exists in our solar system and all of space. What makes Earth different from other planets we know of? Do you think there could be another planet like Earth somewhere in the universe? Discuss your ideas with the class.

Genre

Expository Text is nonfiction that is written to inform, to explain, or to persuade.

Comprehension Strategy

 **Adjusting Reading Speed**

As you read, you may find that some sentences are harder to read than others. Slow down or reread sections you do not understand.

Earth

Our Planet in Space

by Seymour Simon

Focus Questions

What are some of the major features of Earth? How do the sun and moon affect Earth?

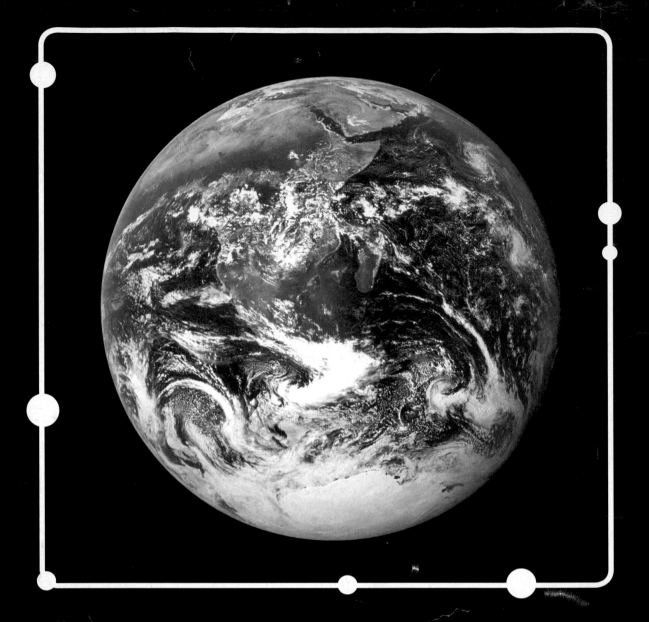

You live on Earth. You may live in a city or in the country. You may live where snow falls or where it never snows at all. But wherever you call home, you live on Earth. We all live on Earth.

Earth is in space. Space is outside the layer of air that surrounds Earth. Here is how Earth looks from miles and miles out in space. The dark places are seas, and the brown places are lands. Some of the seas and lands are covered by white clouds. The large white spot at the bottom is the snow-covered land of Antarctica.

Earth is a planet. A planet is a large world that travels around the sun.

The sun is not a planet. It's a star a million times bigger than Earth. Light and heat come from the sun.

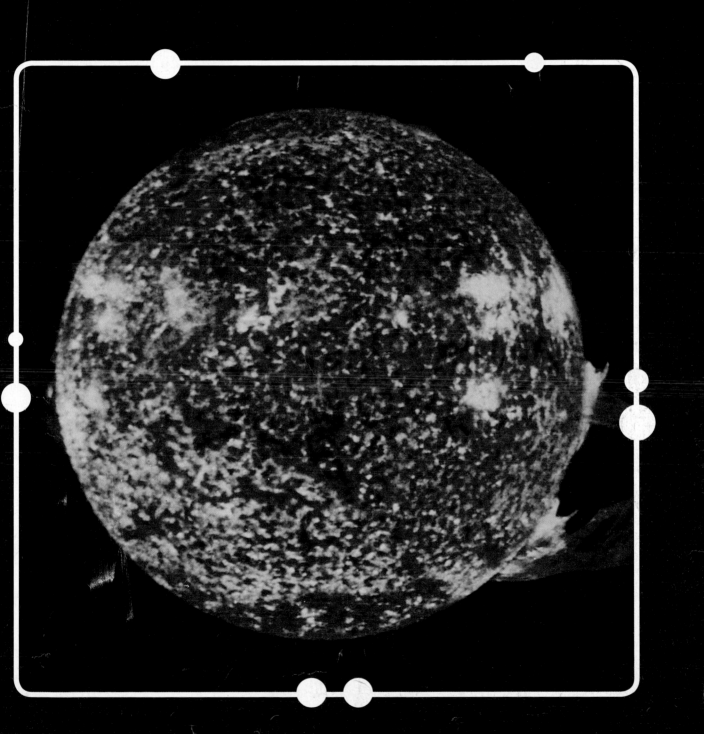

Earth is not the only planet that travels around the sun. Eight planets travel around the sun. Some of the planets are bigger than Earth, and some are smaller. Together, the sun and the planets are called our Solar System.

Here is a picture of the sun and the planets. Ten photographs were used to make this picture. The photographs are not to scale. The sun is six hundred times bigger than all the other planets put together.

If the sun were the size shown in this picture, Jupiter would be about the size of the letter O and Earth would be about the size of the dot at the end of this sentence. The planets are shown in order from the sun. The top four are Mercury, Venus, Earth, and Mars. The next row shows Jupiter, Saturn, Uranus, Neptune, and Pluto. Pluto used to be called a planet. In 2006, a group of astronomers from all over the world decided that Pluto should not be called a planet. Pluto is now called a dwarf planet. Some astronomers think that Pluto is an asteroid or comet rather than a planet. But many people still want Pluto to be called the ninth planet.

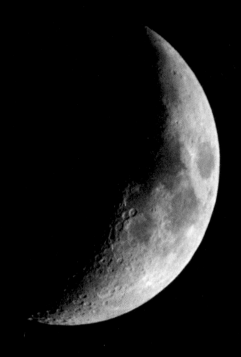

In this photograph Earth's shadow is traveling across the moon. Many years ago, people thought that the Earth was flat, but you can see that the shadow of Earth is of a curve. The shadow helped people learn that Earth is round. Today, scientists photograph and measure Earth from spaceships. They say our planet is shaped almost like a ball. It is very slightly pear-shaped.

In the photograph on the right you can see how Earth looks from the surface of the moon. Light from the sun falls on one half of the Earth at a time. One half of the Earth is light while the other half is dark. From the moon you can see the light side but not the dark side of Earth.

Earth is spinning all the time. It spins like
a giant top. While you are on the light side, it
is daytime. To you, when the light side spins
away from the sun, it looks as if the sun is going
down. Then darkness falls and it is nighttime.
When the dark side spins toward the sun, it
looks to you as if the sun is rising. Light comes
to the side of Earth that has been in darkness
and daytime begins.

But the sun is not moving. It is Earth that is
spinning. We call that motion, Earth's rotation.
It takes one day, or twenty-four hours, for Earth
to rotate once.

While Earth rotates once a day, it also travels around the sun in a path called an orbit. We call that motion around the sun, Earth's revolution. It takes Earth one year, about 365¼ days, to make one complete orbit around the sun.

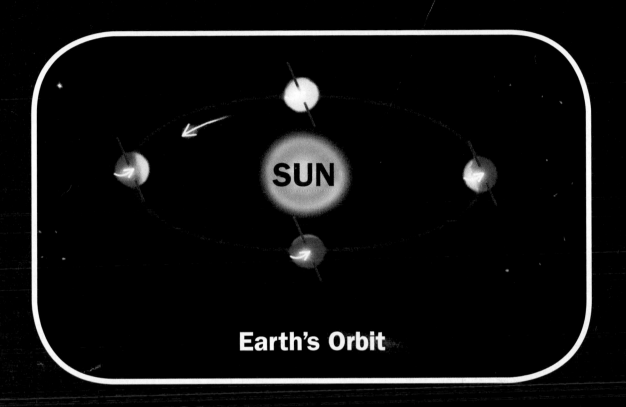

Earth's Orbit

Earth is about 93 million miles from the sun. If Earth were closer, it would broil. If the Earth were farther, it would freeze. The sun is just the right distance for the living things on Earth.

There is no planet that is the same distance from our sun, so there is no planet that has the same temperatures as Earth. As far as we know, Earth is the only one of the planets that has plants, animals, and people.

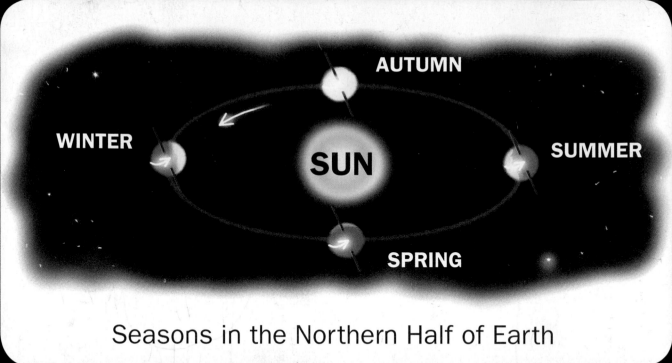

Seasons in the Northern Half of Earth

One half of Earth has winter while the other half has summer. When Earth travels around the sun, it is tilted to one side. For part of the year, the northern half of Earth is tilted toward the sun. When this happens, the northern half of Earth has summer.

At that time the southern half of Earth is tilted away from the sun, so southern places have winter.

The seasons change. Winter changes into spring, which turns into summer, and summer changes into fall, which turns into winter. As Earth travels around the sun, sometimes the north is tilted away, and the northern places become colder. At the same time, the southern half of Earth is tilted toward the sun, and summer comes. As the year goes by, the place where you live on Earth warms up in summer or cools off in winter.

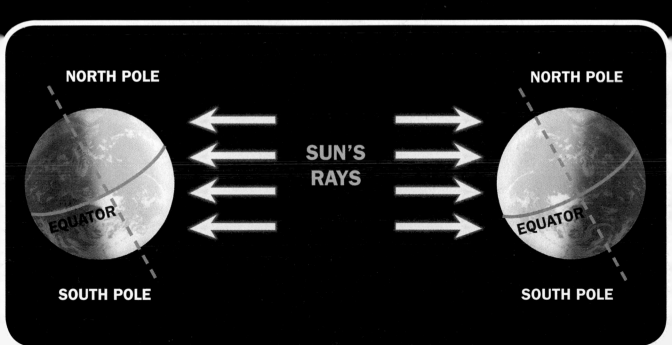

Earth has a blanket of air around it that keeps it from getting too hot or too cold.

The blanket of air is called the atmosphere. Earth's atmosphere is made of gases and bits of dust and water. The atmosphere helps make Earth a planet full of living things. No other planet has an atmosphere like Earth's.

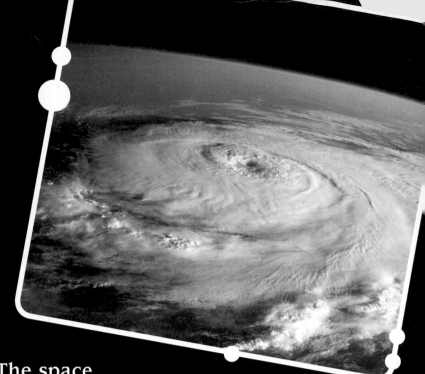

Earth is like a giant magnet. The space around a magnet is called a magnetic field. Earth's magnetic field acts like a shield. It helps protect living things from dangerous radiation from the sun and space that can kill everything on Earth. The magnetic field sometimes makes colored lights you can see in the night sky. These lights are called an aurora. Here is a photograph of an aurora.

The surface of planet Earth is covered with land and water. This is a photograph of lower California. These mountain ranges are mostly barren of vegetation and water, but the white places are caps of snow.

There is much more water than land on the surface of our planet. Oceans cover nearly three quarters of Earth.

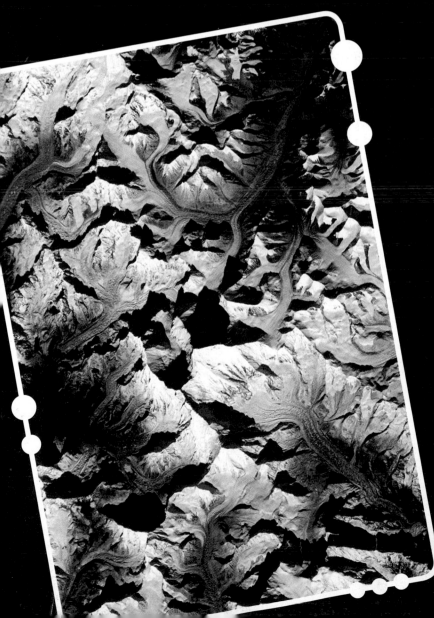

The lands on Earth's surface are always changing. Here is a photograph of the highest mountains on Earth— the Himalayas in Asia. Mountains are pushed up by changes inside our planet. The Himalayas are still rising. The snow-covered mountains are more than twelve thousand feet high. The dark line is a deep river valley. Over many years the river scraped deep into the land.

The surface of the land wears away. In winter, water freezes and becomes ice. The ice breaks up the rock and wears it away. Snow piles up and pushes down on the land. In this photograph you can see how snow and ice have worked to change the surface of the land.

People also change the surface of the land. They farm the land. They dig into the land and use the rocks and minerals they find. This is a photograph of Phoenix, Arizona.

Can you see the ways the land has been changed?

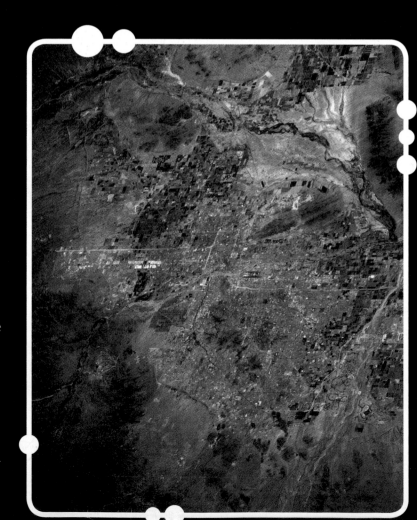

This is New York City. Millions of people live here in thousands of buildings. Yet this great city is just a tiny speck on Earth's surface. To an astronaut on the moon, which is Earth's closest neighbor in space, no signs of people can be seen.

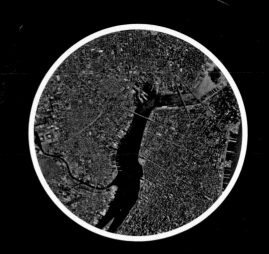

People have dreamed of leaving Earth to explore other worlds in space. We have already landed on the moon. We have sent spaceships to explore the other planets in our Solar System.

We have also found other planets circling far-distant stars. As we learn about these planets, we learn about Earth as well.

All of us travel together through space. Our spaceship is called Planet Earth.

Meet the Author

Seymour Simon

Seymour Simon has loved science and nature since he was a young boy. After going to college and teaching science at an elementary school, he decided to write books for children full time. He has now written over 200 books. Simon's books are popular because he makes learning fun. He makes sure that the information in his books is interesting and easy to understand. Today Simon enjoys spending time with his grandchildren and has even written a few books just for them.

Earth, Moon, and Sun

Theme Connections

Within the Selection

1. How do you feel when you look at pictures of Earth taken from far out in space?

2. The atmosphere protects Earth. What are some ways people can protect and care for Earth?

Across Selections

3. In "The Moon Seems to Change," how is Earth's orbit the same as the moon's orbit?

4. How is Earth's orbit different from the moon's orbit?

Beyond the Selection

5. What does Earth Day mean to you?

6. What kinds of activities could people do to celebrate Earth Day?

Write about It!

Describe the place on Earth where you would choose to have a home.

Remember to look for pictures of Earth to add to the **Concept/Question Board.**

Science Inquiry

Sharp Shades

You have made a good choice! Amber Waves sunglasses are the key to good vision. Our lenses sharpen as well as protect your eyesight.

We use an amber lens because yellow is the color that blocks blue. Blue light waves scatter easily. This creates glare in sunlight or in the lights of an oncoming car. With Amber Waves, you can see objects more clearly—on the ski slopes, on the boat, or in the car. What's more, our glasses block 100% of the sun's rays that can harm your eyes.

Use and Care of Your Sunglasses

Make sure your glasses are the right size for your face. They should not be too large or too small. A poor fit lessens the protective effects of your glasses.

The curve at the end of the temple should rest over your ear. The temple should not press down on the ear. An optician can adjust the curve for the best fit.

Wash your lenses at least twice a week. Use mild soap and warm water to remove dirt and oil. Dry the lenses with a lens cloth or soft cotton cloth. Hold the glasses by the frame with one hand. With the other hand, gently rub each lens. Do not press hard on the lens.

Our lenses are made to resist scratching but are not scratch proof. Do not clean the lenses with paper or clothing, which have coarse fibers. Do not place the glasses with the lenses facedown. Keep your glasses in a case when you are not wearing them.

Think Link

1. How do yellow-tinted lenses reduce glare?

2. What parts of the text are explained with picture symbols?

3. Why do manufacturers include owner's guides and manuals with their products?

Try It!

As you work on your investigation, think about how you can create symbols to communicate messages.

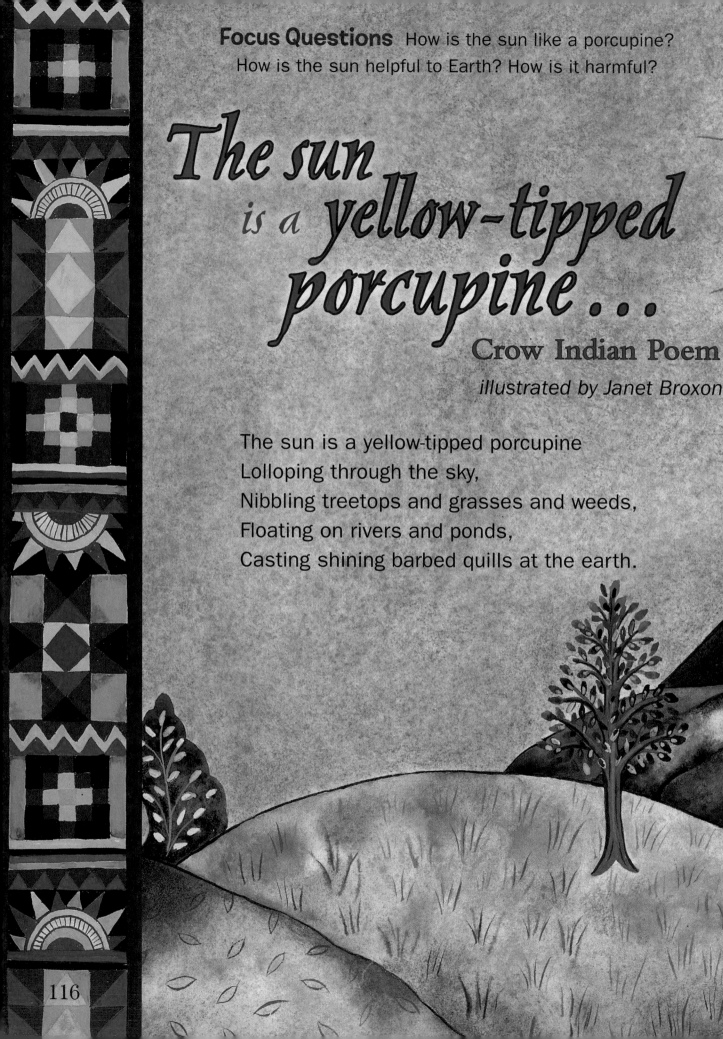

The sun is a yellow-tipped porcupine...

Crow Indian Poem

illustrated by Janet Broxon

The sun is a yellow-tipped porcupine
Lolloping through the sky,
Nibbling treetops and grasses and weeds,
Floating on rivers and ponds,
Casting shining barbed quills at the earth.

THE UNIVERSE

by Mary Britton Miller
illustrated by Stacey Schuett

There is the moon, there is the sun
Round which we circle every year,
And there are all the stars we see
On starry nights when skies are clear,
And all the countless stars that lie
Beyond the reach of human eye.
If every bud on every tree,
All birds and fireflies and bees
And all the flowers that bloom and die
Upon the earth were counted up,
The number of the stars would be
Greater, they say, than all of these.

Test-Taking Strategy: Skipping Difficult Items

Sometimes you will read a test item that seems hard. Skip this item and come back to it later.

Skipping Difficult Items

The best way to work on a test is by doing one thing after another in a way that makes sense. One way is to answer easier items first, then come back to the hard item.

> **Read the questions below. Decide which one seems hard and which seems easy.**
>
> At the end of the story, Chris probably felt
>
> Ⓐ proud. Ⓑ clever.
> Ⓒ happy. Ⓓ tired.
>
> At the end of the story, Chris probably wanted
>
> Ⓐ to explain about the different kinds of clouds.
> Ⓑ to inform the reader about how clouds are formed.
> Ⓒ to show how some clouds are more likely to cause rain.
> Ⓓ to persuade the reader to spend more time watching clouds.

The first question is easier. It has fewer words and asks a question about a character. The second question will take longer to read. You might want to come back to this harder item after you do the easier ones.

Test-Taking Practice

Read the selection "Dusty Earth." Then answer numbers 1 through 4.

Earth is a dusty place. Did you ever wonder where it all comes from? Most dust comes from nearby. Cars riding on dirt roads cause dust. Even people walking on the street make dust. Some dust, however, comes from surprising places.

Dust in your house might come from a desert far away. Researchers from NASA found that dust in Africa could be blown all the way to Florida.

An orbiting satellite watches dust from space. When it is windy, the dust swirls and moves very fast. It goes from one place on Earth to another.

There is another way that scientists know where dust comes from. They test what the dust is made of. Different kinds of dust are made of different chemicals.

Dust can cause a haze in the sky. Haze is like a big, thick cloud that you cannot see through easily. The dust mixes with other kinds of pollution to make the haze.

GO ON

Most of the time, dust is just a nuisance. You have to clean it with a cloth from the top of a table. If there is too much of it, dust can be a real problem. A dust storm happens when a lot of dust blows around. It can cause traffic accidents. Planes cannot fly if there is a bad dust storm. The pilots cannot see, and the dust can cause problems with a plane's engines.

A big dust storm can cause another kind of problem. Some dust contains iron. When the dust falls into the ocean, the iron makes tiny plants grow too fast. They change the color of the water and make it a little red. People call it a "red tide." Red tides can kill fish and hurt other sea animals.

The next time you see dust on your shoes, think about this. That dust might have traveled halfway around the world to get there.

GO ON

Use what you learned from "Dusty Earth" to answer Numbers 1 through 4. Write your answers on a piece of paper.

Test Tips

- Say each answer to yourself.

- Skip difficult items and come back to them later.

1. What does it mean to say that dust is a nuisance?

Ⓐ Wind blows it.

Ⓑ Haze pushes it.

Ⓒ It annoys you.

Ⓓ It bores you.

2. In the article, how does dust travel from one place to another?

Ⓐ Planes carry it.

Ⓑ Waves move it.

Ⓒ Wind blows it.

Ⓓ Haze pushes it.

3. Scientists look at what dust is made of to learn

Ⓐ why dust makes storms.

Ⓑ where dust comes from.

Ⓒ when the dust landed.

Ⓓ who made the dust.

4. A "red tide" is bad because

Ⓐ it can kill fish and hurt other animals.

Ⓑ it can damage a plane's engine.

Ⓒ it can cause big dust storms.

Ⓓ it can affect how satellites work.

Communities across Time

What do you think of when you hear the word *community*? A community can be a geographic location, such as a town or a city. A community also can be the people, or a group of people, who live within the town or city. Where is your community? What was it like 20, 100, or even 1,000 years ago? How has your community changed since its beginning? Let's find out how our communities came to be, how human beings affect the land where we live and work, and how the land affects us!

Theme Connection

Look at the illustration. How many time periods do you see? How has this community changed through the years? What has changed, and what has not changed?

BIG Idea

How has my community changed over time?

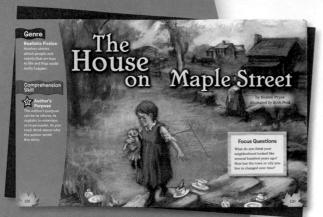

Read the article to find the meanings of these words, which are also in "The House on Maple Street":

- ✦ **settlers**
- ✦ **treasures**
- ✦ **sturdy**
- ✦ **fierce**
- ✦ **trickle**
- ✦ **stump**
- ✦ **crumbling**
- ✦ **burrows**

Vocabulary Strategy

Apposition is when a word or group of words define another word in the same sentence. Use apposition to find the meaning of *sturdy*.

Vocabulary
Warm-Up

The settling of America began in the East and moved west. Landscapes and climates differed across the country. However, settlers in all regions faced some of the same challenges.

Settlers had to choose what to take with them to a new place. Furniture and other large treasures were left behind. The settlers took no more than they needed.

In their new land, settlers had to build a sturdy, or solid, house. They needed homes that could stand up to fierce winds and harsh weather. Choosing the right home site was key. Settlers looked and listened for the trickle of a stream. A close water supply was a big plus.

Many settlers built log cabins. Some early cabins were quite rough, unlike modern log cabins. Shelter was necessary, not style.

Trees had been cut to clear the land. To use it as a field for crops, each tree stump had to be dug from the ground. Farmers hacked at roots until they could pull free the pieces that were crumbling.

Settlers had to learn about wildlife, and whether animals were friends or foes. They learned to look for tracks and animal homes. Where there were burrows, there might be a source of food.

It took a strong will for settlers to succeed, but many of them did. They started with a few simple goods. With these, they built new lives in a new land.

GAME

Making Sentences

Work with a partner to create sentences using the vocabulary words. Choose two words from the list, and challenge your partner to make up a sentence using the two words. Then switch roles. Continue until all of the vocabulary words have been used.

Concept Vocabulary

The concept word for this lesson is **transform.** To **transform** means "to change the form or condition of something." Both human and natural activities can transform an environment. What are some ways that people transform land? What are some ways that land is transformed by natural events?

127

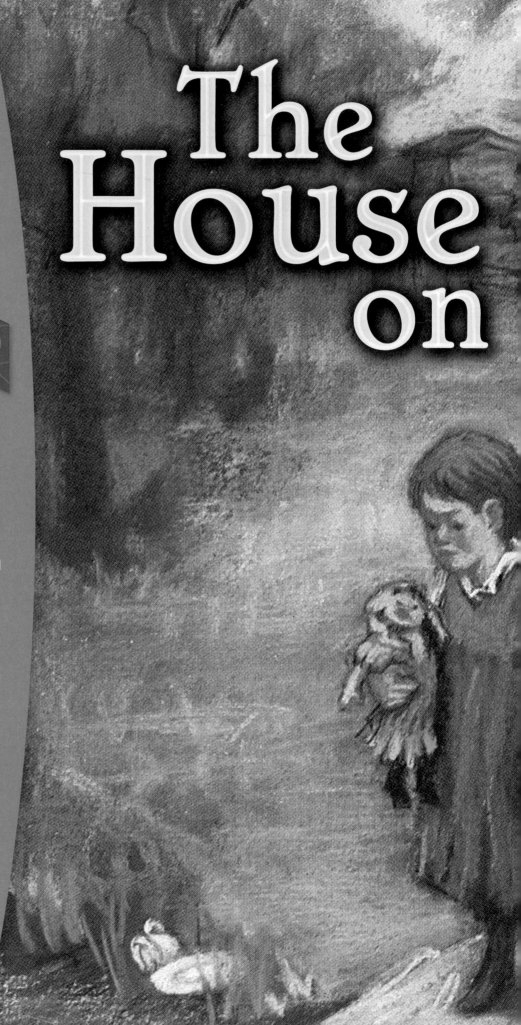

Genre

Realistic Fiction involves stories about people and events that are true to life and that could really happen.

Comprehension Skill

 Author's Purpose

The author's purpose can be to inform, to explain, to entertain, or to persuade. As you read, think about why the author wrote this story.

The House on

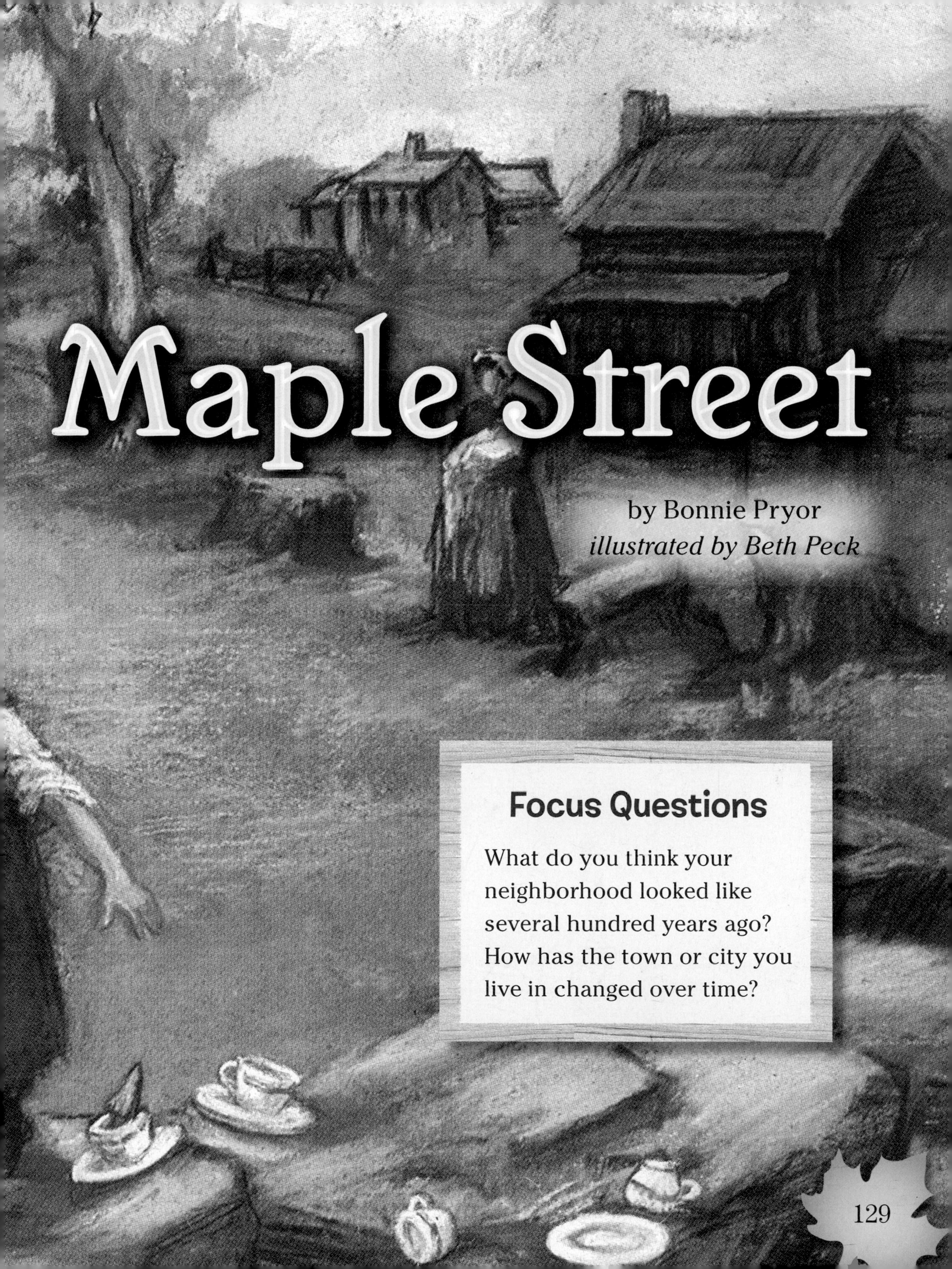

Maple Street

by Bonnie Pryor

illustrated by Beth Peck

Focus Questions

What do you think your neighborhood looked like several hundred years ago? How has the town or city you live in changed over time?

129

This is 107 Maple Street. Chrissy and Jenny live here with their mother and father, a dog named Maggie, and a fat cat named Sally.

Three hundred years ago there was no house here or even a street. There was only a forest and a bubbling spring where the animals came to drink.

One day a fierce storm roared across the forest. The sky rolled with thunder, and lighting crashed into a tree. A deer sniffed the air in alarm. Soon the woods were ablaze.

The next spring a few sturdy flowers poked through the ashes, and by the year after that the land was covered with grass. Some wildflowers grew at the edge of the stream where the deer had returned to drink.

One day the earth trembled, and a cloud of dust rose to the sky. A mighty herd of buffalo had come to eat the sweet grass and drink from the stream.

People came, following the buffalo herd. They set up their tepees near the stream, and because they liked it so much, they stayed for the whole summer.

One boy longed to be a great hunter like his father, but for now he could only pretend with his friends. In their games, one boy was chosen to be the buffalo.

His father taught the boy how to make an arrowhead and smooth it just so, the way his father had taught him. But the boy was young, and the day was hot.

He ran off to play with his friends and left the arrowhead on a rock. When he came back later to get it, he could not find it.

The buffalo moved on, searching for new grass, and the people packed up their tepees and followed.

For a long time the land was quiet. Some rabbits made their home in the stump of a burned tree, and a fox made a den in some rocks.

One day there was a new sound. The fox looked up. A wagon train passed by, heading for California. The settlers stopped beside the stream for a night. But they dreamed of gold and places far away and were gone the next morning.

Other wagons came, following the tracks of the first. The fox family moved into the woods, but the rabbits stayed snug in their burrows until the people had gone.

Soon after, a man and a woman camped along the stream. They were heading west, but the woman would soon have a child. They looked around them and knew it was a good place to stay. The man cut down trees and made a house.

He pulled up the tree stumps left from the fire and planted his crops. The child was a girl, and they named her Ruby and called her their little jewel.

Ruby had a set of china dishes that she played with every day. One day when she was making a mudpie on the banks of the stream, she found an arrowhead buried deep in the ground. She put it in a cup to show her father when he came in from the fields.

Ruby's mother called her to watch the new baby. While she was gone, a rabbit sniffed at the cup and knocked it off the rock. It fell into the tunnel to his burrow, and the rabbit moved away to a new home under the roots of a tree.

Ruby grew up and moved away, but her brother stayed on the farm. By now there were other people nearby, and he married a girl from another farm. They had six children, and he built a larger house so they would all fit.

Now the old wagon trail was used as a road, and the dust got into the house. When his wife complained, Ruby's brother planted a row of maple trees along the road to keep out the dust and shade the house. After the children were grown, he and his wife moved away, but one of their daughters stayed on the farm with her husband and children.

One day the children's great-aunt Ruby came for a visit. She was an old lady with snow-white hair. The children loved to hear her stories of long ago. She told them about the cup and arrowhead she had lost when she was a girl.

After she left, the children looked and looked. But they never found them, though they searched for days.

The town had grown nearly to the edge of the farm, and another man up the road filled in the stream and changed its course. For a while there was a trickle of water in the spring when the snow melted, but weeds and dirt filled in the bed, until hardly anyone remembered a stream had ever been there.

New people lived on the farm. It was the schoolteacher and his family, and they sold much of the land to others. The road was paved with bricks, so there was no longer any dust, but the maple trees remained. The branches hung down over the road, making it shady and cool. People called it Maple Street. Automobiles drove on the road, along with carts and wagons, and there were many new houses.

The house was crumbling and old, and one day some men tore it down. For a while again, the land was bare. The rabbits lived comfortably, with only an occasional owl or fox to chase them. But one day a young couple came walking along and stopped to admire the trees.

"What a wonderful place for a home," said the young woman. So they hired carpenters and masons to build a cozy house of red bricks with white trim.

The young couple lived happily in the house for several years. The young man got a job in another town, and they had to move.

The house was sold to a man and a woman who had two girls named Chrissy and Jenny and a dog named Maggie, and a fat cat named Sally.

The girls helped their father dig up a spot of ground for a garden, but it was Maggie the dog who dug up something white in the soft spring earth.

"Stop," cried Chrissy, and she picked up the tiny cup made of china. Inside was the arrowhead found and lost so long ago.

"Who lost these?" the girls wondered. Chrissy and Jenny put the cup and arrowhead on a shelf for others to see. Someday perhaps their children will play with the tiny treasures and wonder about them, too. But the cup and arrowhead will forever keep their secrets, and the children can only dream.

Meet the Author

Bonnie Pryor

Books and reading have always been important to Bonnie Pryor. As a child, she sometimes got into trouble for reading when she was supposed to be helping around the house or when she was supposed to be sleeping late at night. Pryor says her six children often appear in her stories. She and her husband now live in the country where they care for horses, rabbits, cats, and a dog.

Meet the Illustrator

Beth Peck

Beth Peck studied art at the Rhode Island School of Design, the Art Students League, and the National Academy of Design. Her favorite books to illustrate are those about people from all over the world. She has lived in Wisconsin and New York City. She lives with her husband and a few cats.

Communities across Time

Theme Connections

Within the Selection

1. How do you think the street where you live was named?

2. What kind of changes have taken place in your neighborhood since you have lived there?

Beyond the Selection

3. What are some things you can usually find in a community?

4. How do you feel about being part of a community?

Write about It!

Write a news story about an old tree near your home or school.

Remember to look for newspaper articles about historic sites in your town to add to the **Concept/Question Board.**

Home Tour Celebrates Spanish Heritage

Next week the Board of Realtors will hold its fifth Parade of Homes featuring Spanish-style homes. The tour links the Palos Verdes and Buena Vista Villas neighborhoods.

Homes on the tour reflect the influence of Spanish settlers. Among the first to come to our region, they brought their style with them. True to Spanish form, most homes on the tour are made of stucco. Guests will see homes in many hues. Pale brown and peach are standard shades. Yet crisp, white stucco is just as common.

Such light house tones highlight the red tile roofs. The settlers formed the curved roof tiles by hand. Now made by machine, the tiles still convey a sense of "Old World" Spain.

Admire the courtyard on your way inside. Look for brightly colored tiles on walls and floors. Do not miss the wrought-iron accents in the garden and on the arched front door.

Detailed tile patterns and arches are also inside. Curved doorways and windows create soft lines, contrasting with the straight lines of the ceilings.

Hundreds of advance tickets have already been sold for the tour. To find out more, contact the Board of Realtors.

Think Link

1. A news story answers the questions Who? What? When? and Where? How are they answered here?

2. Name three common features of Spanish villas.

3. Use the above map to answer the following question. In which direction and on what streets will tour visitors travel to get from Palos Verdes Estates to Buena Vista Villas?

Try It!

As you work on your investigation, think about how you can use a map to show your facts.

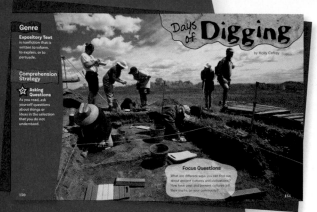

Read the story to find the meanings of these words, which are also in "Days of Digging":

+ beats
+ developed
+ laboratory
+ origins
+ challenge
+ charted
+ ruin
+ customs

Vocabulary Strategy

Context Clues are hints in the text. They help you find the meanings of words. Use context clues to find the meaning of *origins*.

Vocabulary

Warm-Up

Rain beats down on the tree house, but Lena does not mind. This house is where she loves to go on a rainy day.

Lena's is not any typical tree house. It began as a few boards flung across some branches. As time went by, the house developed into something special. It became part library and part laboratory.

Lena gathers leaves and nuts on her walks. Back at the tree house, she studies the specimens. She tries to identify the origins of each piece. From which tree did it drop?

Lena looks at a nut. She now gets to challenge her skill. "Yes, it's just an acorn. But," Lena asks herself, "from which tree?"

Lena has charted, or mapped, the trees on her street. There are blue oaks and black oaks. There are buckeye and ash trees. And there is the lopsided maple tree. Lightning caused the ruin of a few of its large limbs. Each tree is sketched in and labeled on Lena's map.

Lena concludes that the acorn is from a blue oak. Then she puts the nut on the window ledge and waits. Lena is not the only one who knows about this tree. Some squirrels have chosen the same site for their house.

Like many neighbors, Lena and the squirrels have their customs. The routine is always the same. Lena leaves her samples on the ledge, and the neighbors come by for a snack.

GAME

Synonyms

Make a list of the vocabulary words on a sheet of paper. Beside each word, write a synonym for that word. When you and a classmate are both finished, compare the synonyms you came up with for each vocabulary word.

Concept Vocabulary

The concept word for this lesson is *relic.* A **relic** is something that survives from an earlier time or place. A relic can be an object. It can also be an idea or a way of doing things. Your school probably has relics from students and teachers who were there before you. What kinds of things can we learn from relics? Record your ideas in a journal.

Genre

Expository Text is nonfiction that is written to inform, to explain, or to persuade.

Comprehension Strategy

Asking Questions

As you read, ask yourself questions about things or ideas in the selection that you do not understand.

150

Days of Digging

by Holly Cefrey

Focus Questions

What are different ways you can find out about ancient cultures and civilizations? How have past and present cultures left their marks on your community?

The summer sun beats down. You wipe the sweat from your forehead. The sound of a pickax hitting rock carries off into the distance. Your team has been at this dig for three months. Each day, it takes an hour by jeep to get to the site. The water that you drink has to be boiled so that you will not get sick. Within the month, you hope to be back at the museum.

You sit back for a moment, jotting notes in your field book. While you take a break, you watch as the twenty members of the team carry out the excavation. Slowly and carefully, layers of dirt are removed. Every inch of the dig is charted or mapped on paper. Objects are studied before they are removed from the ground. Artifacts are drawn, numbered, and photographed. The artifacts are then examined inside a tent—your makeshift laboratory. Then they are carefully packed so that they can be sent to the museum.

You put your field book down and return to your
work. You use a fine brush to remove the loose
dirt around something that you have found. So far,
the team has found animal bones. The bones are
thousands of years old. The bones have scratches
and marks on them. Your team believes that
humans made the marks. You hope to find the
bones of the humans who you believe lived here
long ago.

The piece that you are working on slowly comes loose. It is a small rock, but it is no ordinary rock. It has sharp edges, which were made by humans. You have found an ancient human tool. It may have even been the sharp tool that made marks on the animal bones. Your heart beats with excitement. Now you know that humans were here.

You tell the rest of your team. Everyone is excited. Within the next few weeks, your team discovers many more tools. Human bones are also found. Who were these people? What were they like? Your team has just begun to find out the history of these people of the past.

Imagine being the first person to unearth an ancient city. Imagine finding the bones of an ancient warrior. Imagine solving the five-thousand-year-old mystery of what happened at a place where all the villagers died at once. Archaeologists get to challenge themselves with many thrilling possibilities of the past.

Archaeology (ancient study) is a science. The archaeologist discovers and studies past human cultures or societies. Each group that is studied has its own values, customs, and beliefs. An archaeologist does research about a culture. He or she studies the artifacts from that culture. He or she also tries to find out when and how the culture developed. This study can take an archaeologist to any place on the planet.

Some archaeologists try to solve puzzling issues. They may try to solve mysteries about a culture's ruin or disappearance. They may try to find out why a culture did certain things. They may try to find out why a culture changed dramatically from its origins. For example, an archaeologist would try to discover why a culture that fished developed into a culture that farmed. What caused the culture to stop fishing? What made them start farming? These questions may be answered through archaeology.

You may wonder why it is so important to learn about our human past. It is important because it teaches us about being human. It shows us how creative and resourceful humans really are—and have been. The past is important because it tells us how we became what we are today. It also explains how and why we have so many different cultures. It teaches us to respect those cultures, and our own.

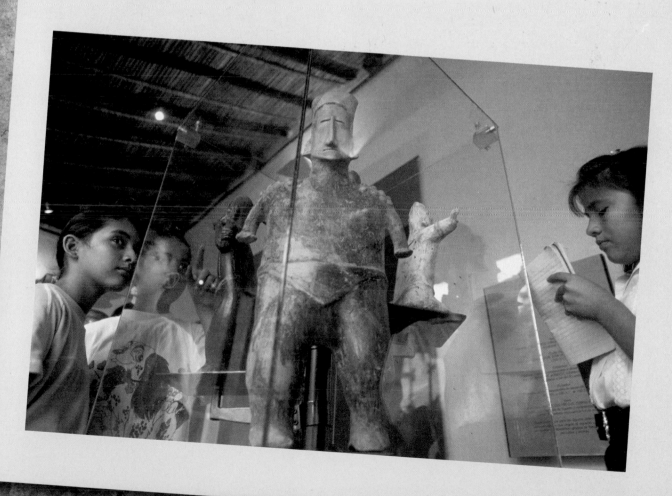

Meet the Author

Holly Cefrey

As a freelance writer, Holly Cefrey writes for a variety of people and publishers. She is primarily known for writing informational books that help children learn about different subjects, such as science and health. Cefrey has won many awards for her writing.

Communities across Time

Theme Connections

Within the Selection

1. If you were an archaeologist, what culture would you like to study? Explain why.

2. How is an archaeologist's work like putting together a jigsaw puzzle?

Across Selections

3. How are Chrissy and Jenny from "The House on Maple Street" like archaeologists?

4. How are artifacts found in "The House on Maple Street" like those found in "Days of Digging"?

Beyond the Selection

5. What are some skills an archaeologist should have?

6. What other jobs involve studying the past?

Write about It!

Describe a modern tool as if it were an artifact discovered at a dig hundreds of years from now.

Remember to record questions about ancient civilizations to add to the **Concept/Question Board.**

John Muir: Mountain Man

"Everybody needs beauty as well as bread . . ."

These are the words of nature lover John Muir. Muir is well known for his work to preserve America's wild lands. They are places he knew well and held dear.

Muir was born in Scotland in 1838. He came to the United States when he was 11 years old. He worked long, hard days on a farm in Wisconsin.

Muir had an awful accident as a young man. A sharp tool pierced his eye, and Muir lost his vision. In a few months, his sight came back. Muir felt he had a new chance at life. He resolved to enjoy the sights and places he treasured. He longed to be close to nature.

"None of Nature's landscapes are ugly so long as they are wild."

Muir traveled widely. In time, he came to California. He fell in love with the beauty of Yosemite. He made his home in the valley. Muir explored the mountains, cliffs, and waterfalls. He strolled through the forests and meadows.

Muir wrote books and essays about Yosemite. He stressed the splendor of the land and wildlife there. His work drew a great deal of attention.

Muir grew alarmed by changes he saw. Grazing sheep wrecked the hills. Lumber firms cut down huge, old trees. Muir fought to save the valley from ruin.

Muir made a plea to Congress to make Yosemite a national park. He charted the areas that should make up the park. They agreed.

Muir also helped start a private group to protect the region. The Sierra Club was formed in 1892. It carries on Muir's ideals to this day.

Think Link

1. Look at the quote at the beginning of the article. What did John Muir mean by this statement? What does this tell you about Muir's view of nature?

2. How did John Muir's accident change him?

3. What did John Muir do to protect the wilderness of Yosemite Valley?

Try It!

As you work on your investigation, think about how you can use quotes to tell more about a topic.

Read the article to find the meanings of these words, which are also in "Earthquake! The 1906 San Francisco Nightmare":

✦ shattered
✦ section
✦ rumble
✦ clerk
✦ damaged
✦ frames
✦ tough
✦ exactly

Vocabulary Strategy

Word Structure is when parts of a word help you understand the word's meaning. Use word structure to find the meaning of *exactly*.

Vocabulary
Warm-Up

The best way to stay safe in an earthquake is to be prepared. Survival can depend on having a good plan. Here are some helpful safety tips.

- When the ground starts shaking, duck and seek cover. Get under a strong desk or table, and hold on to one of its legs. Cover your eyes to protect them from shattered glass.

- Stay away from tall, heavy furniture that could fall on you. Get to a section of your home that has no windows or large light fixtures.

- When the shaking stops, check to see if you are hurt. Have a first aid kit handy to treat wounds.

- Listen for the rumble of aftershocks. More tremors will likely roll through after the first quake. Once again, you should duck, cover, and hold on.

- Be sure you have a fire extinguisher that works. A clerk at the hardware store can help your family choose the best model for your home.

- Find out from a builder whether your house is bolted down. In the past, major earthquakes damaged house frames less when they were attached to their base.

- Fasten things that might fall and cause harm, such as a television or bookcase. Put tough latches on cupboard doors.

- Practice earthquake drills with your family. Have a plan that each person knows exactly how to follow. Choose a safe place in each room where you can duck, cover, and hold on.

GAME

Write a Riddle

Make a riddle for each of the vocabulary words. For example, for the word *rumble,* you might write, "I am much louder than a mumble, and when you hear me, you know the earth might crumble." Exchange papers with a classmate, and solve each other's riddles.

Concept Vocabulary

The concept word for this lesson is **community.** A **community** is a group of people who live in the same area or have a shared interest. People in a community often help each other. They also work together to make decisions about their neighborhood. In your journal, write about some of the benefits of being part of a community.

Fire!

Thomas Chase had stayed away from flying stones and sparking power lines to get to work. Now he helped people onto ferryboats.

The gas had caught fire and flames covered the city. Horses couldn't get through the broken streets. Firefighters had to get to the fires on foot. When they reached a fire there was no water to put it out. The pipes had burst.

Lloyd Head's mother sewed bags together to make a tent. The family camped outside. They were afraid their house would fall. People watched rescue workers try to put out the flames with coats and brooms.

Soldiers blew up buildings to stop the fire from spreading.

170

A Shattered City

Three days later, the fire was out. The shaking had stopped. The beautiful city of San Francisco was a mess.

The death count was about 700. People who study history, however, say as many as 3,000 people died. About 225,000 people were hurt. The earthquake destroyed 490 city blocks. Over 25,000 buildings had fallen. It would take millions of dollars to rebuild San Francisco.

Without warning, much of San Francisco had been flattened like a sand castle hit by a wave. How did it happen? How does any earthquake happen?

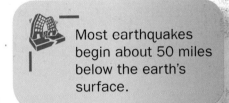

Most earthquakes begin about 50 miles below the earth's surface.

171

What Is an Earthquake?

The city had been hit by shock waves. These waves start below the earth's surface, where there are large pieces of rock. These rocks are called tectonic plates. The plates fit against one another like a puzzle.

Each plate floats on hot liquid rock. Sometimes plates push against each other. If the plates slip while they're pushing, shock waves occur. These waves travel up and can cause the ground to move.

An earthquake is usually followed by aftershocks. The aftershocks occur as the rocks get into their new positions. The 1906 San Francisco Earthquake had 135 aftershocks.

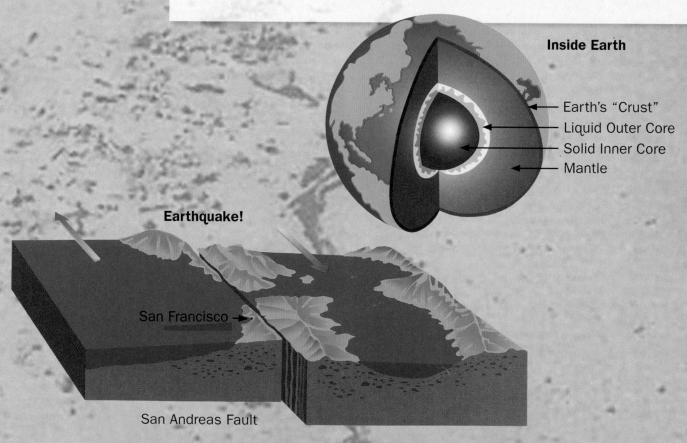

Inside Earth

Earth's "Crust"
Liquid Outer Core
Solid Inner Core
Mantle

Earthquake!

San Francisco

San Andreas Fault

An earthquake is caused by movements within Earth's crust.

Whose Fault Is It?

Each year, half a million earthquakes occur around the world. Most are harmless. About a hundred are big enough to cause trouble, mainly those near cities.

Earthquakes usually occur along weak places in the earth's crust called faults. San Francisco sits on the San Andreas Fault. This fault stretches along part of the state. It causes most of California's many earthquakes.

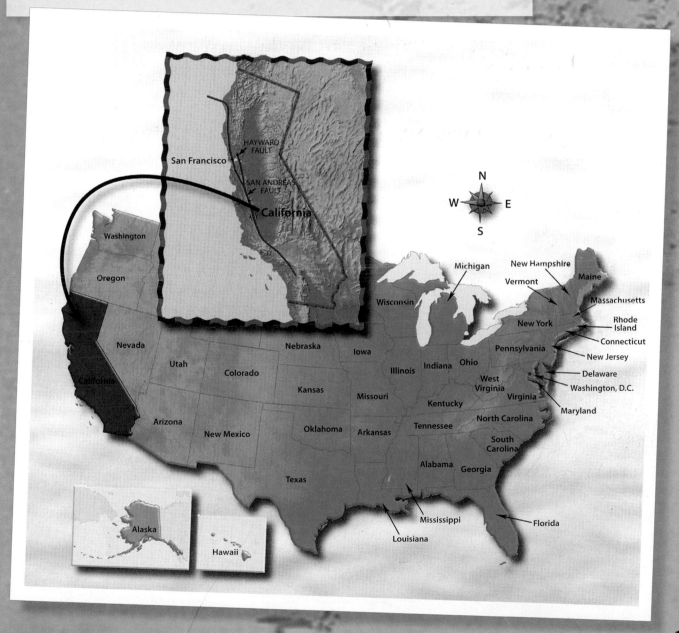

173

Take a Number

Since 1906, scientists have learned a lot about earthquakes. They have special tools to help them. One is a seismograph. It's used to record the movement of the earth during an earthquake.

Scientists give each earthquake a number on the Richter Scale. This scale measures the power of an earthquake. The highest numbers go to the biggest earthquakes.

The scale uses numbers and parts of numbers to measure power exactly. If an earthquake is rated "five point two," that means its number is 5.2. It has more power than an earthquake rated 5.1.

The biggest earthquake in the world measured 9.5 on the Richter Scale. This earthquake occurred in Chile in 1960.

Movements of the earth show up as heavy lines on a seismograph chart.

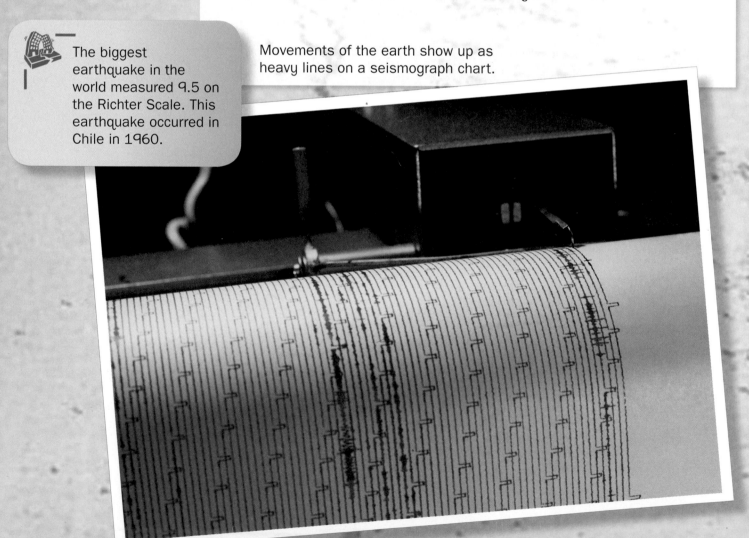

174

America's 10 Strongest Earthquakes on Record*			
Rank	Location	Date	Magnitude
1	Prince William Sound, Alaska	March 28, 1964	9.2
2	Andreanof Islands, Alaska	March 9, 1957	9.1
3	Rat Islands, Alaska	February 4, 1965	8.7
4	East of Shumagin Islands, Alaska	November 10, 1938	8.2
5	New Madrid, Missouri	December 16, 1811	8.1
6	Yakutat Bay, Alaska	September 10, 1899	8.0
7	Andreanof Islands, Alaska	May 7, 1986	8.0
8	New Madrid, Missouri	February 7, 1812	8.0
9	(Near) Cape Yakataga, Alaska	September 4, 1899	7.9
10	Fort Tejon, California	January 9, 1857	7.9

* From the United States Geological Survey

 The San Francisco Earthquake of 1906 would be number 17 on this list. It hit the Richter Scale at 7.8.

America's Biggest Shake-ups

The 1906 San Francisco Earthquake wasn't the biggest earthquake to ever occur. It was, however, the most harmful earthquake in American history.

It caused so much damage because it hit a big city with lots of buildings and people. Earthquakes that hit places with few people and buildings don't cause as much harm, even if they have more power.

Looking for Clues

Days later, Thomas Chase was safe at his mother's house in Oakland, California. Lloyd Head's family was still camping outside. Thousands of others were in tents in the city's parks. They hung signs with names like "Camp Thankful." They were glad to be alive.

Scientists studied photos and maps of the places hit. Workers hunted through the fallen buildings and homes. They were looking for ideas to help make a safer city. They found that buildings on soft land were damaged more than buildings on solid rock. They learned the fire had caused more problems than the earthquake.

The moon also has "earthquakes." These "earthquakes" don't happen often and they aren't strong.

By 1910, many buildings in San Francisco had been rebuilt.

A New San Francisco

After the earthquake, the city made new building rules. The rules were very tough for buildings on soft ground. Tall buildings were made to move with earthquake shocks instead of falling to pieces. Most new buildings had to have steel frames.

New water pipes that could bend easily were put to use. These pipes would be less likely to burst. New gas lines were made more bendable, too.

San Francisco did not put these new rules into effect all at once. The city, however, was ready to welcome visitors to the 1915 World's Fair.

The tectonic plates along the San Andreas Fault slide against each other about as slowly as a fingernail grows.

A poster from the 1915 World's Fair

177

San Francisco Hit Again!

In 1989, another large earthquake shook the city. One place it hit was San Francisco's Candlestick Park. It was before the start of a World Series game. Millions of Americans watched on TV.

This earthquake measured 6.9 on the Richter Scale. This time the city was more prepared. Buildings shook but most did not fall. There was, however, some damage. Parts of the San Francisco-Oakland Bay Bridge fell. A section of the freeway in Oakland fell, too. Forty-two people were killed. Power was knocked out. Fires started around the city. Again, the most damage happened to buildings on soft land.

Damage from the 1989 earthquake cost about 6 billion dollars.

The Future

Scientists think another big earthquake might strike San Francisco in the next 30 years. More than 1,000 earthquake stations are on the lookout for shock waves along California's fault lines. If it seems like an earthquake is about to happen, people can be warned. Families have emergency supplies of food and water. Kids in school practice safety moves such as hiding under a strong table.

Earthquake study in America began because of the 1906 San Francisco Earthquake. Now we know much more. We can't stop an earthquake, but we can live through one.

Every year about 500,000 earthquakes occur. Only about 100 cause damage.

Meet the Author

Lynn Brunelle

Bringing the fun of science to children is a goal for Lynn Brunelle. All of her scientific experiments involve items that kids can find at home. In addition to writing her own books, she has written for Bill Nye, the Science Guy, whose TV show appears on PBS. She won an Emmy Award for her writing on this show. Brunelle lives in Seattle, Washington, with her husband and two children.

Communities across Time

Theme Connections

Within the Selection

1. How do you prepare for emergency situations at home and at school?

2. What can people learn from a tragedy like an earthquake?

Across Selections

3. How are scientists who study earthquakes like the scientists in "Days of Digging"?

4. How are they different?

Beyond the Selection

5. Why do people continue to live in places where there have been earthquakes?

6. How does a tragedy bring a community closer together?

Write about It!

Describe a time when people in your city or town worked together.

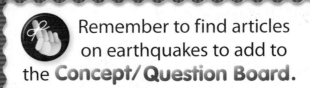

Remember to find articles on earthquakes to add to the **Concept/Question Board.**

Shear Joy!

"Shepherd" is not a job title often heard these days. However, they do still exist. Darryl Ray tells us about his California sheep ranch.

Q: How did you get started as a sheep rancher?

A: The ranch has been in my family for about 150 years. When I was growing up, I wanted to get away and try something else. I lived in the city for a while, but I found that I missed the ranch. So I came back, and I really love the work.

Q: How has the business changed over time?

A: Right after my ancestors settled here, in the late 1850s, there was a big need for wool. It was used to make uniforms for the Civil War. The sheep business was a great success back then. The demand for wool hasn't always been as strong, but there has been enough need to keep the ranch going.

One change in the last ten years or so is the call for organic wool. More and more people want natural products.

This is a growing market for us right now.

Q: What makes wool "organic"?

A: There are some tough rules, but it mostly means the wool is free of chemicals. The sheep feed in fields that have not been sprayed with pesticides for at least three years. And the sheep cannot be dipped in pesticides. Also, they have to have plenty of room to graze.

Q: What do you like most about your job?

A: The best part is that I get to spend a lot of time outside. It also makes me proud to keep up the family tradition.

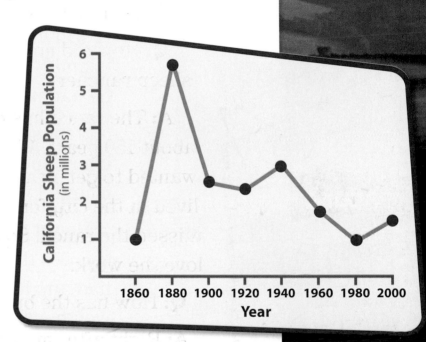

Think Link

1. Why was the Ray family's sheep ranch so successful when it started?

2. Why is the demand for organic wool growing?

3. When was the sheep population in California the highest?

Try It!

As you work on your investigation, think about how you can use a line graph to show your facts.

183

Read the story to find the meanings of these words, which are also in "The Disappearing Island":

+ sheltered
+ voyage
+ acres
+ toppled
+ ripples
+ claim
+ tide
+ eroding

Vocabulary Strategy

Word Structure is when parts of a word help you understand the word's meaning. Use word structure to find the meaning of *eroding*.

Vocabulary
Warm-Up

Raini peered out from his sheltered nook beneath the palm fronds he had lashed together. "Today," he thought, "I will voyage to the other side of the island." There were still acres of land he had not yet explored.

"I must stay positive," Raini commanded himself. "I will get off this island. I will make my way back home."

He set off on his investigation. It seemed like hours passed before he had any luck, but what he found was worth waiting for. A small wooden boat lay ahead of him!

Raini hurried toward the boat, but he toppled in the sand. The faster he tried to go, the more he fell. Would he ever reach it? He struggled forward.

Finally, Raini came to the boat and began to inspect it. He moved his hands along the ripples in the worn wood. There was trouble—a large gash near the bow. The back of the boat seemed to be in good order, though. Raini believed he could patch the hole. He did not know who owned the boat, but he decided he would claim it.

"The tide is in," thought Raini. "I need to leave soon, while the water is high!" However, as Raini packed the gash with shrubbery and mud, it seemed to grow. This hole he could not fix started eroding his hopes of ever getting off the island.

Suddenly, Raini heard a voice. Who could it be? He strained to hear. "Raini! Raini!" someone called urgently. It was his mother's voice! "Raini," she said, "it's time to wake up! You'll miss the bus if you don't get ready soon."

GAME

Writing Sentences

Use each vocabulary word in two sentences. First, use the word in a sentence that asks a question. Then use the word in a sentence that is a statement. Write your sentences on a sheet of paper.

Concept Vocabulary

The concept word for this lesson is **property. Property** is land that a person owns. What makes some property worth more than other property? How does a property's location affect its value? Discuss your ideas with the class.

Genre

Realistic Fiction involves stories about people and events that are true to life and that could really happen.

Comprehension Skill

 Cause and Effect

As you read, think about what causes certain events to happen.

The
DISAPPEARING
Island

by Corinne Demas

illustrated by Ted Lewin

Focus Questions

What physical or environmental changes could cause a community to disappear? What do communities do to survive major changes in their environments?

For my ninth birthday my grandma gave me a small box. Inside was a perfect sand dollar and a note. The note said:

To celebrate your birthday we will voyage out to the disappearing island where I found this sand dollar when I was just your age.

"How can an island disappear?" I asked.

Grandma laughed. "When I take you out to Billingsgate Island, Carrie, you'll see," she said.

I'd been all around Wellfleet Harbor in Grandma's boat, but this time we were going to go farther out, into Cape Cod Bay, just the two of us, farther than I'd ever been before.

Grandma's boat is named *Aphrodite,* after the goddess of love who first rose out of the sea foam. It's painted the blue of the sea on the outside and the blue of the sky on the inside.

The next day we rowed out to *Aphrodite* in a rubber boat so small our legs were in a tangle.

We clambered aboard *Aphrodite,* and Grandma hooked the rubber boat to the mooring. To get the old outboard motor started she had to pull the rope nearly ten times. Her arms are all muscles from clamming and swimming and pulling. We put on our life jackets, and I sat up on the bow and pretended I was a figurehead on one of the old ships that used to come into Wellfleet Harbor. Water sprayed me, but it was a hot day so I didn't mind.

When the tide is high in Wellfleet Harbor, the water is way over my head. When the tide is low, it just comes up to my middle. Grandma has a tide chart on her wall. It's like a calendar for the sea. There's low tide and high tide twice a day, and every day it's an hour different. The tide was going out now. A cormorant was drying out its feathers on a rock that hadn't been there an hour before. When we rode out beyond the sheltered part of Wellfleet Harbor, the waves got higher and I went to sit in the back of the boat with Grandma.

"I don't see any island," I said.

She passed me the binoculars. "Keep looking straight ahead," she told me. "At high tide it is completely covered by water. It begins to appear as the tide goes out."

Finally we got close enough so I could see it: a flat stretch of beach out in the middle of the sea. We pulled into a cove, and Grandma anchored *Aphrodite*. We waded to shore, carrying our lunch basket and beach blanket.

We laid out the blanket on a high sandy spot surrounded by rocks—the foundation for the old lighthouse, Grandma said. Then we went off to explore the island.

There were no buildings, no trees, not even a blade of grass. Just sand. The sand was all in long ripples made by the waves as the tide had gone out. I ran as far as I could run without stopping to catch my breath. Grandma ran beside me.

"A century ago, this island was a mile long," Grandma explained. "This was a busy fishing community, and there were thirty-five homes here and a school. There were meadows and gardens. When the sea started eroding the island, people moved off and took their houses with them. When I was a little girl, my dad used to take me out here to go clamming. There was more of the island than there is now, but no one lived here anymore."

We were the only ones on the island except for the gulls and the terns. There were shells everywhere: jingle shells and quahogs, razor clams and channeled whelks. Mussels, tiny as ants, covered the stones in the acres of tidal pools. They looked like black fur.

I found a broken brick, half buried in the sand. One side of it had been charred.

"This was from someone's chimney," Grandma said.

"May I keep it?"

"Sure. The sea would claim it soon enough."

We hiked back to our blanket, and nearby I saw a strange, rusty creature that looked like the backbone of a whale.

"It's the metal spiral staircase from the old lighthouse, lying on its side," Grandma told me. It was too big for us to carry back to safety on the mainland.

"That was the second lighthouse out here. The first one toppled into the sea. They built this one farther inland and they built it out of brick. They thought it would last forever, but the sea kept taking more and more of the island. They built a big breakwater out of rocks, but the sea just came around it."

Grandma pointed to a curve of gray rocks that were covered with barnacles that looked like white lace.

"That's what's left of the breakwater," she said. "Just around the time I was born, the last lighthouse keeper moved off the island. They built a tower with an automatic light, and that winter the big brick lighthouse was knocked down by the sea in a storm. Now, the light tower is gone as well."

I lay back on the blanket and closed my eyes. The hot sun made everything swimming and orange under my lids. While I listened to Grandma talk, I imagined it was a hundred years ago.

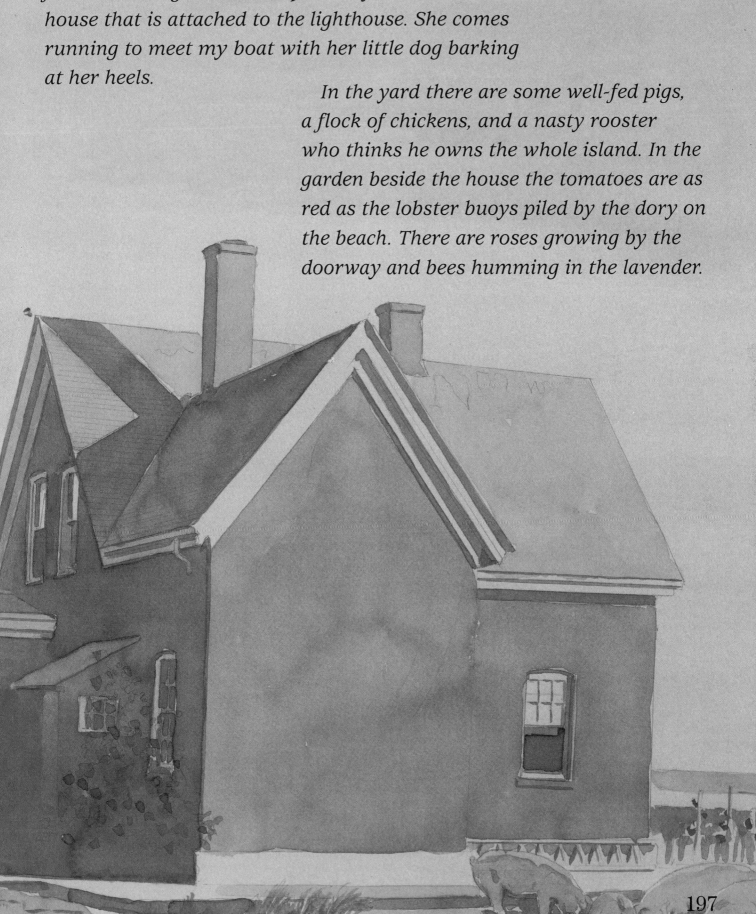

I've come to the island to visit my friend whose father is the lighthouse keeper. They live in the brick house that is attached to the lighthouse. She comes running to meet my boat with her little dog barking at her heels.

In the yard there are some well-fed pigs, a flock of chickens, and a nasty rooster who thinks he owns the whole island. In the garden beside the house the tomatoes are as red as the lobster buoys piled by the dory on the beach. There are roses growing by the doorway and bees humming in the lavender.

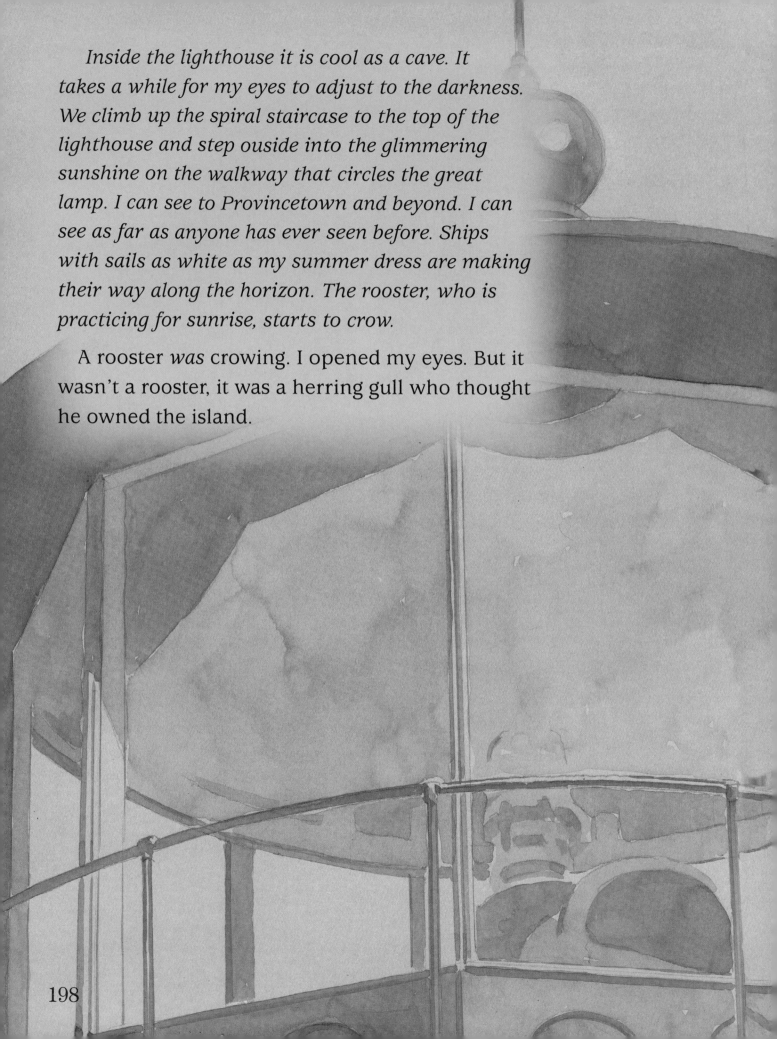

Inside the lighthouse it is cool as a cave. It takes a while for my eyes to adjust to the darkness. We climb up the spiral staircase to the top of the lighthouse and step ouside into the glimmering sunshine on the walkway that circles the great lamp. I can see to Provincetown and beyond. I can see as far as anyone has ever seen before. Ships with sails as white as my summer dress are making their way along the horizon. The rooster, who is practicing for sunrise, starts to crow.

A rooster *was* crowing. I opened my eyes. But it wasn't a rooster, it was a herring gull who thought he owned the island.

In the basket Grandma had packed sandwiches and leftover birthday cake from my party the day before. She lit a candle, and the wind and I blew it out together. Grandma sang "Happy Birthday Plus One."

"Someday," she said, "this island will be completely gone, and you'll tell your granddaughter how you came out here and picnicked on it at low tide."

"I'll show her the brick as proof," I said.

Now the tide was coming back in. It moved slowly at first, as if making up its mind, and then it started claiming the edges of the beach.

Grandma stroked the smooth sand beside her.

"In this modern world people can do almost anything," she said. "We cut canals and build long bridges and dam rivers. We've tamed almost everything. I'm glad that we haven't completely tamed the ocean, too. What I love about a place like this is that it reminds us that nature still can have its way once in a while."

Grandma stood up. "Time to get going," she said.

We each took a corner of the beach blanket and let it flap free of sand in the wind. Then we folded the blanket together, like partners in a square dance. When our hands came together, Grandma kissed my knuckles and my nose.

The tide was coming in faster now, eating up the beach, eating up the island. We waded out to *Aphrodite*. Grandma started the engine in two tries, and we went chugging off. I looked back as Billingsgate Island began to disappear in the distance, and in the sea. The spot where Grandma and I had had our picnic would soon be underwater. Where the chickens once pecked for grain thrown out by the lighthouse keeper's little girl a hundred years ago, fish would peck at plankton.

By the time *Aphrodite* was back at her mooring in Wellfleet Harbor, Billingsgate Island was gone, a secret beneath the waves.

Meet the Author

Corinne Demas

Corinne Demas is an author, a college English professor, and an editor. She has written two novels, a number of short stories, a memoir, and several books for children. Demas spends her summers near the ocean in Cape Cod, Massachusetts, which is where many of her books take place.

Meet the Illustrator

Ted Lewin

When he was young, Ted Lewin knew he wanted to be an illustrator. He began his career by illustrating for adventure magazines and has since become a fulltime children's book illustrator. Lewin grew up with his parents, a brother, a sister, a lion, an iguana, and a chimpanzee. To pay for college, he worked as a wrestler during the summers. Lewin's book illustrations are often inspired by what he sees in his travels.

Communities across Time

Theme Connections

Within the Selection

1. How would you feel if everyone in your community had to leave?

2. What do you think you will remember about your community when you are older?

Across Selections

3. How are changes to the land in "The Disappearing Island" like those in "Earthquake!"?

4. How are the changes different?

Beyond the Selection

5. What can people do to make sure places that have disappeared are not forgotten?

6. What museums have you visited or would you like to visit?

Write about It!

Describe a souvenir you have from a place that is special to you or your family.

Remember to bring articles about how people cope with the effects of nature to add to the **Concept/Question Board.**

Keeping Track

March 18

Today we went to "Railfest" in Fillmore, CA. It is a fair they have each year. I did not think I would enjoy it that much, but it turned out to be fun. I got to ride an old-fashioned steam train, which was cool. I even liked learning about the history of the town.

The railroad is really important to Fillmore. In fact, it is the reason Fillmore exists. The Southern Pacific Railroad built tracks through here in the late 1800s. There was a train station here, helping the area to grow into a town. The town was named after one of the railroad managers.

It is neat that they keep the old railroad cars. I guess a lot of moviemakers like them too. Mom and Dad said that hundreds of movies have been filmed here!

The train took us past some nice farms and citrus groves. At one of the stops, we got off the train and toured a citrus ranch.

There were acres and acres of lemon trees and orange trees. It seems like a nice place to live.

Back in Fillmore, we walked around the town. I like that they have kept a sense of the way things were when the town got started. Maybe I will find out more about the history of my hometown!

Two more days of spring break. Tomorrow, we voyage to Phoenix, AZ. I wish we could take a train!

Think Link

1. How did the town of Fillmore get its start?

2. Why is it helpful to have a standard way to abbreviate state names?

3. How can you tell that history is important to the people of Fillmore?

Try It!

As you work on your investigation, think about how you can use state abbreviations when you take notes.

Read the article to find the meanings of these words, which are also in "What Ever Happened to the Baxter Place?":

+ installed
+ seasonal
+ produce
+ particular
+ featuring
+ necessities
+ expire
+ discount

Vocabulary Strategy

Word Structure is when parts of a word help you understand the word's meaning. Use word structure to find the meaning of *featuring*.

Vocabulary

Warm-Up

On summer weekends, a taste of the country comes to town. The farmers' market is on! Goods are trucked in fresh from the fields.

Vendors line the streets at dawn. They get set up for the day. Tables and temporary booths are installed. Seasonal produce is arranged in neat stacks. There are berries, melons, peppers, and corn.

Soon shoppers start to arrive. They fill their bags and baskets with goods. Some roam the market in no particular order. Others head straight for their preferred booths. They do not want to miss out. A lot of things sell fast at the farmers' market.

Pies and other baked goods are for sale too. These items might be

displayed on elevated plates. Sellers try to entice buyers by featuring the sweet treats. It is a plan that works!

Fresh eggs are sold and packed with care. They are placed in cartons with dividers. This way, the fragile shells will not knock against each other and crack.

Not all of the items for sale are necessities. Although cut flowers are not for eating, they make a meal more pleasant. Handmade quilts may not be as warm as those sold in stores, but they can make a cold night cozier.

Crowds thin as the sale is about to expire. It is time to pack up. Some farmers offer discount prices on the things that remain. They would rather sell their goods for less than haul the stuff home.

GAME

Flash Cards

Make a set of flash cards with the vocabulary words. Write the word on one side and its definition on the other side. Use the flash cards to review the vocabulary words and definitions. Then ask a classmate to use the cards to quiz you.

Concept Vocabulary

The concept vocabulary word for this lesson is **development. Development** means "growth or change." The development of land is when it is changed by adding new buildings. Talk about ways that development can be both good and bad for a community.

Realistic Fiction involves stories about people and events that are true to life and that could really happen.

Comprehension Skill

☆ **Main Idea and Details**

As you read, look for details that help show the main idea of the story.

Focus Questions

Who makes the decisions about how communities change? What are the advantages and disadvantages of using farmland to build more buildings?

What Ever Happened to the Baxter Place?

by Pat Ross

illustrated by Roger Duvoisin

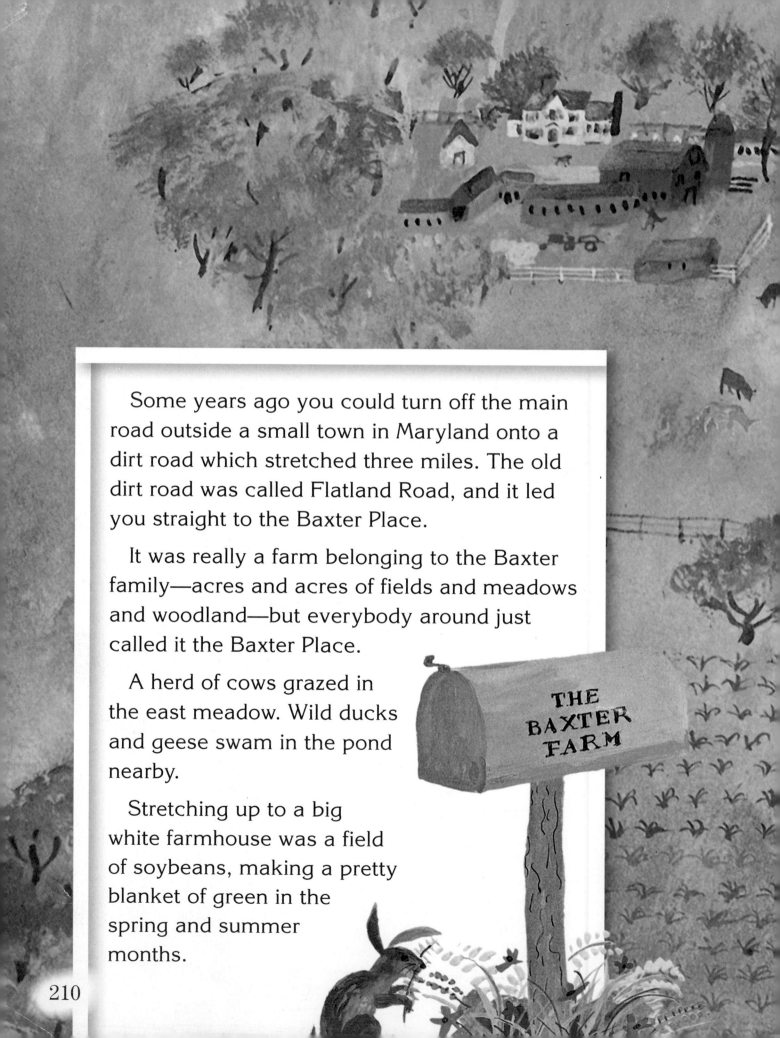

Some years ago you could turn off the main road outside a small town in Maryland onto a dirt road which stretched three miles. The old dirt road was called Flatland Road, and it led you straight to the Baxter Place.

It was really a farm belonging to the Baxter family—acres and acres of fields and meadows and woodland—but everybody around just called it the Baxter Place.

A herd of cows grazed in the east meadow. Wild ducks and geese swam in the pond nearby.

Stretching up to a big white farmhouse was a field of soybeans, making a pretty blanket of green in the spring and summer months.

THE BAXTER FARM

The Baxter Place spread out over nearly three hundred acres. The south field—the biggest and flattest—was planted in rotation with corn one year and barley the next. The rolling east field was well-suited for alfalfa, giving three cuttings each year. The west field, the smallest stretch, was reserved for crops the Baxters might want for their own, with surplus going for sale.

The fields were divided by woods, like nature's markers.

There were four in the family. Sara Baxter was a big, strong woman with a friendly way, and Pete Baxter was a tall and wiry man with skin toughened and tanned from being outdoors all year round. Sue Ann, the older child, seemed to take after her mother's side of the family. Last there was young Pete, named after his dad, but everybody called him Pee Wee. It's said he was so tiny when he was born that he fit in a shoe box, so Pee Wee they called him, and the name stuck.

The Baxter Place was a business—a farm business. It was also a way of life.

Nothing kept Pete Baxter from the work in the fields or in the big dairy barn that had milking stalls for twenty cows at a time. Pete knew every crop, every one of their hundred cows by name, and everything that happened on the farm. For him, farming was more than any regular full-time job, and he liked being outdoors every day all year round.

Sara Baxter raised chickens in a chicken house. During the laying season, she collected about a hundred eggs every day, then drove them to town to Hammil's Country Market to be sold. She also grew vegetables, and those that didn't get eaten right away got canned and

preserved for the long winter or taken to the market along with the eggs. Sara kept careful records of everything that was bought or sold for the farm. She was not only the farm's bookkeeper but also the business-minded one in the family.

Jim and Wally were the hired hands—farmers who work at farming other people's land. Jim was a crackerjack repairman when the tractor and equipment broke down—which was more often than he liked. And Wally knew the planting seasons like the back of his hand. Folks said he could smell a late spring frost in the air. Both Jim and Wally came every morning at six sharp and often stayed till late in the evening. They had worked with Pete for fifteen years.

Sue Ann did her chores every morning before the school bus came up Flatland Road. She cleaned the calves' stalls, fed the chickens, helped with the milking, and set the table for breakfast—which came *after* chores.

Pee Wee, being younger, got away with a little less in the way of work. He was in charge of feeding the three big watchdogs and an untold number of cats, cleaning the chicken house, and helping Sara set out breakfast for everyone.

All the folks around those parts said the Baxter Place was the prettiest, neatest farm they'd ever seen, and the Baxters were some of the nicest folks they knew. Luckiest, too. And they were right—until the day the man from the market stopped by.

Jess Hammil owned the farmers' market where Sara took her eggs and produce to be sold. Sara, Pete, and Jess had all been in grade school together, so they went way back. Jess came to see the Baxters the day he learned the lease on his small vegetable market in town wasn't going to be renewed. A fancy new building was going up in its place, and he sure couldn't afford those rents.

Now, he figured if he could buy his own land—and not rent—something like this wasn't likely to happen again. He had saved the cash, so maybe the Baxters would be willing to part with that small west field. With those twenty-five acres, Jess could not only have his market, he could also grow much of his own seasonal produce instead of always depending on other farmers. The field was right off the main road from town, so people would be likely to stop and buy.

It was true that particular piece of land was what you might call extra. Sara and Pete had always thought they would save it for Sue Ann and Pee Wee. But Sue Ann was headed for forestry college in a year and planned to move later on to the mountains where her work would be. And Pee Wee, young as he was, had his

heart set on being a mathematician, and claimed he was allergic to field work—which certainly seemed to be true!

Jess's being an old friend and all helped the Baxters decide to sell. Also, Sara thought it would be kind of nice to have a market for her sales so close by. They shook hands and made a deal.

Within a year, Jess opened a brand-new market. He planted his land with seasonal produce crops. When word got around that the state was planning to widen and resurface Main Road, Jess knew this meant even more business for him.

Pete and Sara figured they'd not only made some money to pay the bills more easily, but they'd also done a favor for a friend.

Every year for the past five, Emma Price from Homestead Realty Company had made her call on the Baxters. Every year it was the same: Emma's real estate company was interested in purchasing and developing their meadow and woodland area around the pond. Would they consider selling? The offer would be handsome.

Every year they greeted Emma Price politely, but their answer had always been a firm no. They needed the meadow for the cows. And how could they part with the woods and pond? Besides, they didn't need the money. So each year they bade Emma good-by with the same answer.

But one year, things were a little different. The corn harvest that fall had been a total loss. There had been too much rain during planting time and a dry spell just when they needed rain. Corn was their livelihood, and without the crop's sale the bills would go unpaid. Sara figured they could barely pay for the farm's necessities that year. They also owed the bank a mortgage on the house and the land plus money they had borrowed for seed and a new tractor.

They insisted they would not part with the meadow, pond, and woods. Still, they didn't like getting into debt any more if they could help it. Would the Homestead Realty Company consider the rolling east field? they asked. Emma Price was pleasantly surprised and said yes right away.

It was the toughest decision they'd ever had to make together.

Would the company please save some of the trees when they made room for houses? Sue Ann asked. Emma Price assured her they'd make every effort to do just that. Would the Baxters get the best price, even though the east field was the company's second choice? Sara and Pete asked. Emma quoted them a price. Would the new people have children his age? Pee Wee asked. Everyone laughed nervously. Pete quickly figured out loud that they could use the front soybean field for alfalfa, too. There would just be less of a soybean crop, and they would have to sell off some of the older cows in the herd, but the fifty milk-producing cows would not go hungry.

Hurting with the pain of parting with their good land, but having to, the Baxters signed the east field over to Emma Price's company. Homestead Realty paid them without delay. In turn, the Baxters paid for their bad year and looked forward to better ones.

Soon bulldozers were clearing the land, leaving pitifully few of the trees, going against what Emma Price had promised. But it was not all bad, the Baxters told themselves and each other. When the noises and smells of building began to die down, the new houses looked pretty and comfortable, and the people who moved into them seemed friendly enough. It was just strange to see the old alfalfa field planted with so many houses.

Several years of good crops did follow and things seemed to be almost back to normal, even though more and more houses were being built all around. Sue Ann won a partial scholarship to forestry college. Everybody was proud of her, but missed her a lot.

Pee Wee had just started high school when the milking problem came up. Each morning he'd pitch in to take Sue Ann's place. Jim and Wally still arrived at the crack of dawn, but Jim was getting on in years, and it seemed to take him longer to get the cows milked than it used to. Besides, a lot of the local farmers were putting in new automatic equipment— milking parlors, they

called them, with an elevated stall for each cow and tubes leading right to the main tank. The Baxters still relied on the old methods. Not that they wouldn't have changed over. But the cost of the new setup was more than they could swing. So, for a while at least, Pee Wee did his best to help out. Wally never missed a day, but he was no longer up to heavy work, so Sara pitched in more often.

Still, it got harder and harder to compete with the milk production of neighboring farmers who had installed milking parlors to handle larger herds in less time than it took the Baxters. Milk sales were barely bringing in enough to cover costs, so it wasn't long before the Baxters began to sell off the rest of their herd.

Finally, only five cows grazed in the meadow. The milking barn was practically empty. And even though the Baxters didn't have their herd, they took comfort in knowing that the milk and butter on their kitchen table was not store-bought, but still their own.

The following spring George Stillwell came to see Pete and Sara Baxter about using the pond and meadow area for sports land. He didn't want to *buy* the land—which pleased the Baxters, as they'd made up their minds they'd never part with the pond. George Stillwell proposed leasing the area for eight years.

He would put up what he called a "rustic cabin" and, in turn, rent it out to hunters during the fall and winter gunning seasons.

Pete figured that was a good enough deal. The pond was a safe distance from the housing development. Besides, the whole area filled up with hunters during the duck and goose seasons anyway. The Baxters had always let some hunters on their land, so a few more couldn't do much harm, except for the noise. And without actually giving up the land, they would be paid for it. This would fill the hole in their pockets left by the loss of milk money, and would help to fill Pee Wee's college savings account. So Sara, too, reluctantly agreed.

In the next year, the cabin, only a little bigger than the Baxters had expected, went up. They could live with a few hunters for eight years.

Pee Wee, now Petie to everyone except his family, went off to engineering school a whole year ahead of his graduating class. This came as no great surprise to the Baxters, and his ambitions made them proud.

Jim retired officially, but still came around to tinker with the machinery and complain how the new tractor wasn't up to the old model.

Again, things returned almost to normal. Pete and Sara had a smaller place, but it was plenty for them and Wally to handle. They still had the big south field for corn and barley, and the front field for other crops. Sara had her chickens and her garden. Life on the farm was different, what with the

changes and Sue Ann and Pee Wee away most of the year. Perhaps now things would stay put for a while. And they did in fact—for some time.

But things once set out of order never quite stay put for long.

One day something happened that the Baxters found hard to understand. Jess Hammil sold out to a developer, a big developer.

Jess's country market and his land were bulldozed to make Main Shopping Mall, featuring a giant supermarket, a discount drugstore, a dress boutique, a chain department store, and countless other small shops.

Not long after this, Homestead Realty Company made the Baxters an offer on the big south field. This time they didn't *have* to sell, but Wally was about to retire and Pete

and Sara were no longer up to heavy work. They could look for new hired hands, but it just didn't seem the same. The offer was tempting, so they finally accepted.

One thing led to another. The man who'd rented the pond made an offer to buy now that the lease was about to expire. Since the pond and meadow would never be the same again, what with a shopping center bordering it, the Baxters could see little reason to hold onto it. It had lost almost all its meaning for them.

After the sale to George Stillwell—the most profitable and the most heartbreaking for the Baxters—the cabin was turned into Rustic Manor Motor Lodge and Tennis Club almost overnight.

The Baxter Place was not even half of what it had been not too many years before. But the trees—those that were left—still acted as dividers, trying hard to keep the Baxter Place separate.

Sara and Pete still had the front field leading up to the old farmhouse. In the early years, they had had to struggle hard just to make the place pay for itself. Now they had some money in the bank. That was something.

Folks couldn't still say the Baxter Place was the prettiest, neatest place around—not the way it had gotten so divided up and changed. But folks could still say the Baxters were some of the nicest folks they'd ever known. And they were. That had not changed. But so many things *had*.

"What ever happened to the old Baxter Place?" somebody asked. And nobody could quite say. Not even the Baxters.

Meet the Author

Pat Ross

Pat Ross began writing and drawing as hobbies. After finishing school, she discovered that she had a gift for writing children's stories. Many of Ross's books focus on the spirit and challenges of young girls. The books in her M & M book series have won many awards.

Meet the Illustrator

Roger Duvoisin

Roger Duvoisin was born in Switzerland and became a citizen of the United States in 1938. Throughout his career, he wrote over 40 children's books and illustrated more than 140 books altogether. Duvoisin loved drawing animals, which seemed to come to life through both his words and drawings. His *Happy Lion* books were very popular. For these, Duvoisin was the illustrator and his wife, Louise Fatio, was the author.

Theme Connections

Within the Selection

1. How would you feel if you were one of the Baxter children?

2. How has land in your area been changed to meet the community's needs?

Across Selections

3. How are the Baxters like Grandma in "The Disappearing Island"?

4. How are they different?

Beyond the Selection

5. Why do some communities protest plans to build strip malls and superstores in their areas?

6. Why do some people want these kinds of stores nearby?

Write about It!

Describe a farm that you have visited or read about.

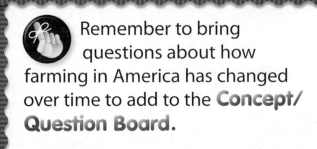

Remember to bring questions about how farming in America has changed over time to add to the **Concept/Question Board.**

Hoover Dam

The Colorado River is mighty. It once flowed completely wild. In spring, the river would flood its banks. This caused great damage to farms and towns by the river.

In summer, some parts of the river dried up. People, plants, and animals could not get the water they needed to live. These were harsh times.

What could be done about the floods and droughts? The government came up with a plan. Today it is known as Hoover Dam.

It took five years and thousands of workers to build Hoover Dam. It was finished in 1936. The dam sits on the border of Arizona and Nevada, but it affects far more than these two states.

Behind the dam, a lake was formed. It was named Lake Mead. The huge lake meant there would be a steady supply of water. This changed life in the Southwest.

A large amount of produce is grown in California. These crops need a great deal of water. Much of that water comes from Lake Mead.

The dam provides more than water. It makes energy too. A power plant was installed at the base of the dam. It turns the force of falling water into electric power.

Now the river still rages. The desert still burns hot and dry, but Hoover Dam is there to help.

Think Link

1. How did Hoover Dam and Lake Mead change life in the American Southwest?

2. Look at the pie chart. What can you infer about California's population compared with those of Arizona and Nevada?

3. Some people are opposed to building dams. What are some negative effects a dam could have on the environment?

56% California

25% Arizona

19% Nevada

Distribution of Electrical Power from Hoover Dam

Try It!

As you work on your investigation, think about how you can use a pie chart to show your facts.

Focus Questions What does it mean to discover a new place? What animals do you suppose lived in your neighborhood before people settled it?

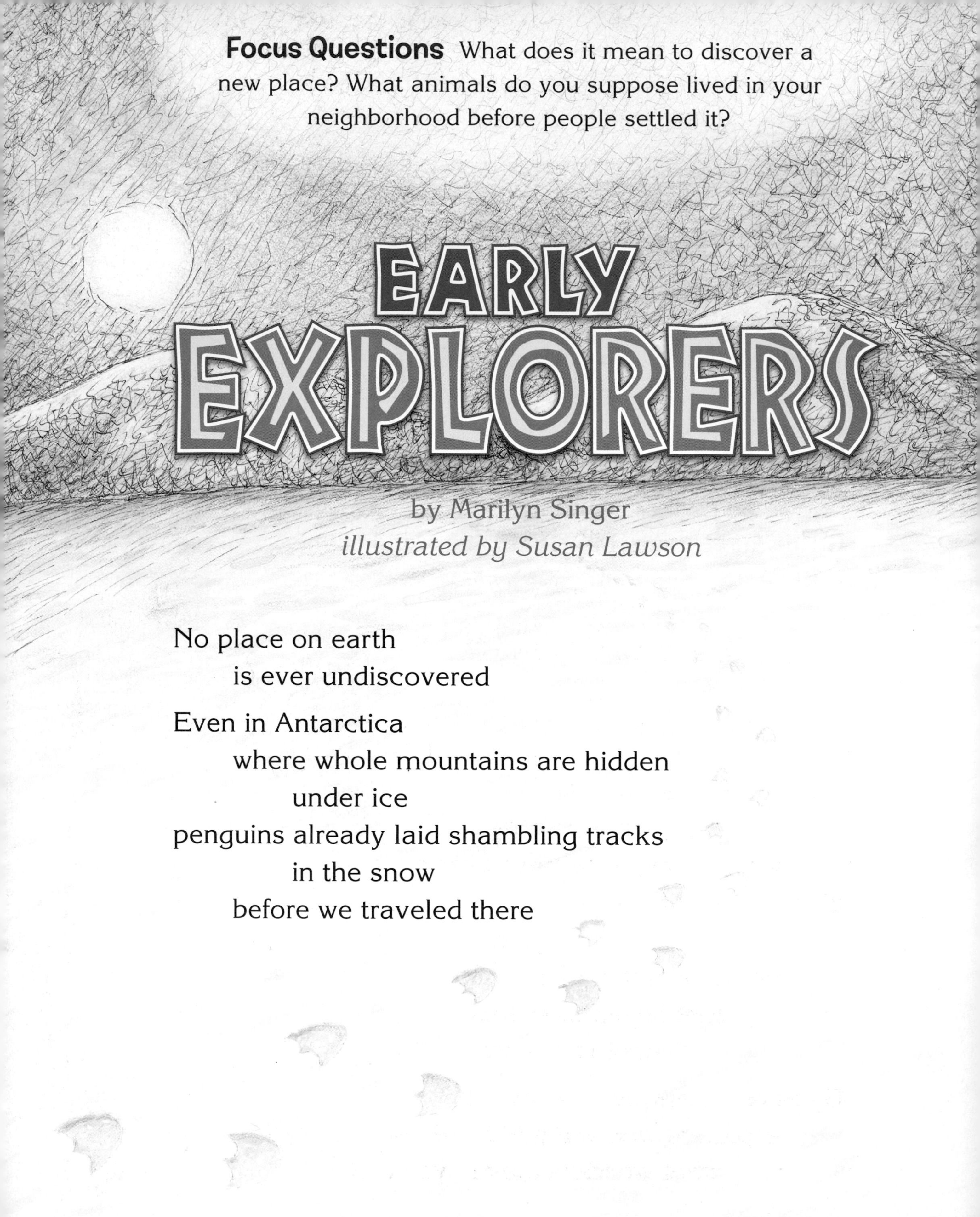

EARLY EXPLORERS

by Marilyn Singer

illustrated by Susan Lawson

No place on earth
    is ever undiscovered
Even in Antarctica
    where whole mountains are hidden
        under ice
penguins already laid shambling tracks
        in the snow
    before we traveled there

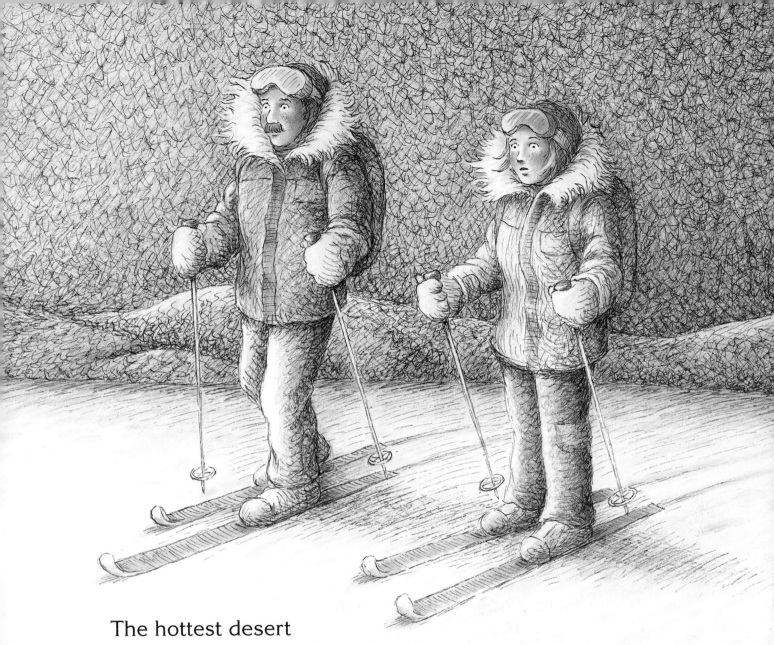

The hottest desert
    the deepest jungle
  where none of us have ever been
all have been crossed
    and crossed again
  by wings whirring or silent
    feet furred or scaled
      hoofed or bare

By adventurers we will never know
  explorers who will never tell us
    what wonders they have seen

Focus Questions What are your favorite places to play outside? How can you help care for your community?

Caring for the World

by Jane Whittle
illustrated by Se Hee Jung

Save me a clean stream, flowing
to unpolluted seas;

lend me the bare earth, growing
untamed flowers and trees.

May I share safe skies
when I wake, every day,

with birds and butterflies?
Grant me a space where I can play

with water, rocks, trees, and sand;
lend me forests, rivers, hills, and sea.

Keep me a place in this old land,
somewhere to grow, somewhere to be.

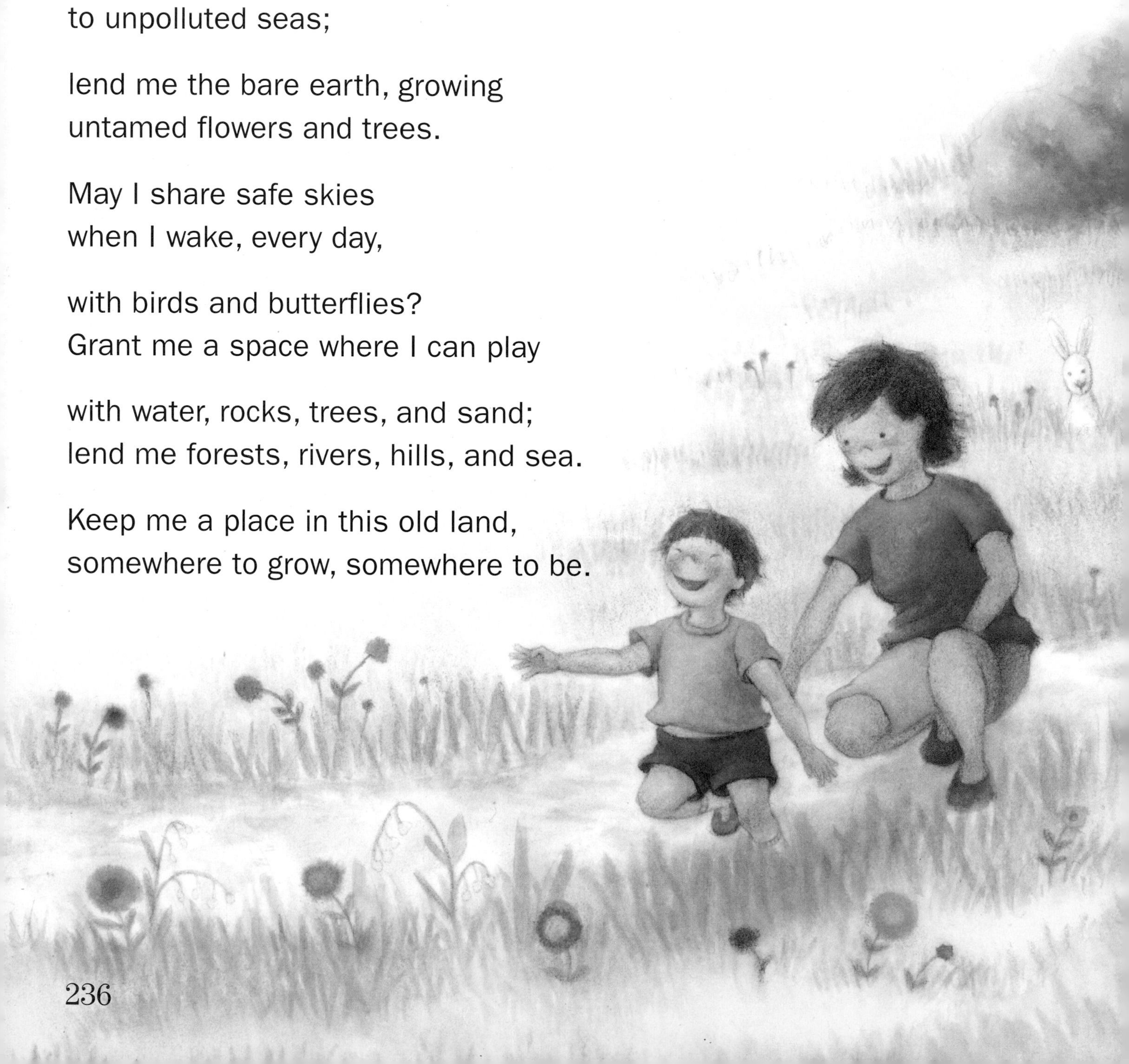

Referring to a Story to Answer Questions

Sometimes you will read a story on a test. Do not memorize the story. Just read it, and try to understand what you read. Look back at the story to answer the questions about it.

Read this story. Use the story to choose the correct answer.

The steep climb to the top of the mountain is not easy. It gets colder as you go higher. The air at the top is also thinner. It is harder to breathe. Some people feel faint or dizzy when they get to the top.

All of these make the climb to the top of the mountain hard EXCEPT

(A) The climb is steep.

(B) There are many steps.

(C) It gets colder as you go higher.

(D) The air is thinner.

Compare each answer to the story. Which answer is NOT mentioned in the story? It mentions all of the answers except the second one. The story says nothing about steps.

Remember to always use the story to answer questions.

Test-Taking Practice

Read "Losing Our Beaches." Then answer numbers 1 through 4.

Ocean states like Florida, New Jersey, Texas, and California are known for their beaches. People come from all over to enjoy them. Beaches also protect us from ocean waves. These beaches, however, are changing. Some are wearing out.

When a beach wears out, it is called *erosion*. This is often caused by natural events, such as a storm. Big waves can push sand from one beach to another or to the bottom of the ocean.

Wind can cause beaches to wear out. A strong wind can blow sand away from a beach. Wind erosion happens more slowly than water erosion.

When an earthquake happens in the ocean, a huge wave can form. This dangerous wave is called a *tsunami*. It can be over 30 feet tall. A wave this big can wash away an entire beach.

Beaches can also wear out if we do not take care of them. In the past, sand was taken from beaches and used for building.

Another way people can cause beach erosion is by hurting sand dunes. A dune is a sandy hill. Sand dunes are sometimes made flat to build houses. Grass and bushes growing on sand dunes might be taken away. This changes the beach so that wind and water can damage it more quickly.

Many people build their homes by the beach. Over time, the land around the homes may wear away. The houses fall apart and people are forced to move. These people can often build new houses farther back. Sometimes, however, they must move away. There is not enough beach left to build a house.

There are things people can do to prevent beach erosion. One is to keep or make more sand dunes. Another is to build walls or put big stones in the water. These will change the way that waves hit the beach. The sand will stay on the beach, and people will be able to enjoy it for a long time. It may not always work, but sometimes it does.

Use what you learned from "Losing Our Beaches" to answer Numbers 1 through 4. Write your answers on a piece of paper.

Test Tips

- Read the directions carefully.

- Look back at the story to find the answer.

- Read each question carefully.

1. The last paragraph of this story mainly tells

Ⓐ how sand dunes are created by wind.

Ⓑ what a tsunami can do.

Ⓒ what causes beach erosion.

Ⓓ how to prevent beach erosion.

2. What is the author's main purpose for writing "Losing Our Beaches"?

Ⓐ To compare new and old beaches

Ⓑ To teach about beaches wearing out

Ⓒ To explain why beaches are important

Ⓓ To warn beach visitors about tsunamis

3. How are storm erosion and tsunami erosion DIFFERENT?

Ⓐ Tsunamis are more natural than storms.

Ⓑ Tsunamis are more powerful than storms.

Ⓒ Tsunamis happen more often than storms.

Ⓓ Tsunamis happen in more places than storms.

4. When erosion takes sand away from a beach, where does it go?

Ⓐ To other beaches or the bottom of the ocean

Ⓑ To rivers that empty into the ocean

Ⓒ To deserts far from the ocean

Ⓓ To dunes beside the ocean

Storytelling

Everyone loves stories. Stories can be true or make believe, and can be read aloud or silently. Stories can be told and retold and passed down through many generations. We learn from the stories we hear. We learn about our families, as well as our culture and the cultures of others. We also can become the storytellers by telling our stories to others.

Fine Art
Theme Connection

Look at the sculpture **Storyteller** by Joe Cajero Jr. What type of story do you think the woman is telling? Are the children interested in the story? How do they show it?.

Joe Cajero Jr. (b. 1970/Native American). **Storyteller.** 1994.
Clay.

Read the article to find the meanings of these words, which are also in "Tomás and the Library Lady":

+ eager
+ cot
+ lap
+ package
+ setting
+ gulps
+ howling
+ borrow

Vocabulary Strategy

Word Structure is when parts of a word help you understand the word's meaning. Use word structure to find the meaning of *package*.

Vocabulary
Warm-Up

If you plan to go camping, make sure you are prepared. The correct supplies can make your trip a success. Even if you are not eager to sleep outside, you might find you enjoy it.

First, you want to have a good, sturdy tent. Get to your campsite a few hours before night falls. This will give you time to set up the tent while you can see what you are doing!

You also want to have a comfy bed. Many sleeping bags are made to keep campers warm and dry. However, if sleeping on the ground is not your style, bring a small cot.

Be sure you have plenty of clean water. You do not want to be forced to lap tainted water from a rusty pump. Play it safe, and bring bottled water.

Do not forget to toss in a package of cocoa mix. As the sun is setting, you can sit by a campfire with family and friends. Between gulps of cocoa you can sing songs and tell stories. You might hear wild animals that are howling their own tunes!

A flashlight is another tool you will need. Suppose you get lost at night. A light glaring in the dark can be a signal for help. Also, remember to pack extra batteries for the flashlight.

Do not rush out and buy costly supplies for your first trip. Try to borrow as much as you can from friends. Then, if you have a good time, you can start to gather your own set of camping gear.

GAME

Flash Cards

Make a set of flash cards with the vocabulary words. Write the word on one side of the card and its definition on the other side of the card. Use the flash cards to review the vocabulary words and definitions. Then ask a classmate to use the cards to quiz you.

Concept Vocabulary

The concept vocabulary word for this lesson is *imagination.* **Imagination** is the ability to form mental images, or pictures. Storytellers often use words that create pictures in the audience's imagination. Talk about how you use imagination to better understand a story.

Tomás

and the Library Lady

by Pat Mora

illustrated by Raul Colón

Focus Questions:

In what ways can a story be told? What places in the world can you travel to in your mind while reading a story or poem?

It was midnight. The light of the full moon followed the tired old car. Tomás was tired too. Hot and tired. He missed his own bed, in his own house in Texas.

Tomás was on his way to Iowa again with his family. His mother and father were farm workers. They picked fruit and vegetables for Texas farmers in the winter and for Iowa farmers in the summer. Year after year they bump-bumped along in their rusty old car. "Mamá," whispered Tomás, "if I had a glass of cold water, I would drink it in large gulps. I would suck the ice. I would pour the last drops of water on my face."

Tomás was glad when the car finally stopped. He helped his grandfather, Papá Grande, climb down. Tomás said, *"Buenas noches"*—"Good night"—to Papá, Mamá, Papá Grande, and to his little brother, Enrique. He curled up on the cot in the small house that his family shared with the other workers.

Early the next morning Mamá and Papá went out to pick corn in the green fields. All day they worked in the hot sun. Tomás and Enrique carried water to them. Then the boys played with a ball Mamá had sewn from an old teddy bear.

When they got hot, they sat under a tree with Papá Grande. "Tell us the story about the man in the forest," said Tomás.

Tomás liked to listen to Papá Grande tell stories in Spanish. Papá Grande was the best storyteller in the family.

"*En un tiempo pasado,*" Papá Grande began. "Once upon a time . . . on a windy night a man was riding a horse through a forest. The wind was howling, *whooooooooo,* and the leaves were blowing, *whish, whish . . .*

"All of a sudden something grabbed the man. He couldn't move. He was too scared to look around. All night long he wanted to ride away. But he couldn't."

"How the wind howled, *whooooooooo*. How the leaves blew. How his teeth chattered!

"Finally the sun came up. Slowly the man turned around. And who do you think was holding him?"

Tomás smiled and said, "A thorny tree."

Papá Grande laughed. "Tomás, you know all my stories," he said. "There are many more in the library. You are big enough to go by yourself. Then you can teach us new stories."

The next morning Tomás walked downtown. He looked at the big library. Its tall windows were like eyes glaring at him. Tomás walked around and around the big building. He saw children coming out carrying books. Slowly he started climbing up, up the steps. He counted them to himself in Spanish. *Uno, dos, tres, cuatro . . .* His mouth felt full of cotton.

Tomás stood in front of the library doors. He pressed his nose against the glass and peeked in. The library was huge!

A hand tapped his shoulder. Tomás jumped. A tall lady looked down at him. "It's a hot day," she said. "Come inside and have a drink of water. What's your name?" she asked.

"Tomás," he said.

"Come, Tomás," she said.

Inside it was cool. Tomás had never seen so many books. The lady watched him. "Come," she said again, leading him to a drinking fountain. "First some water. Then I will bring books to this table for you. What would you like to read about?"

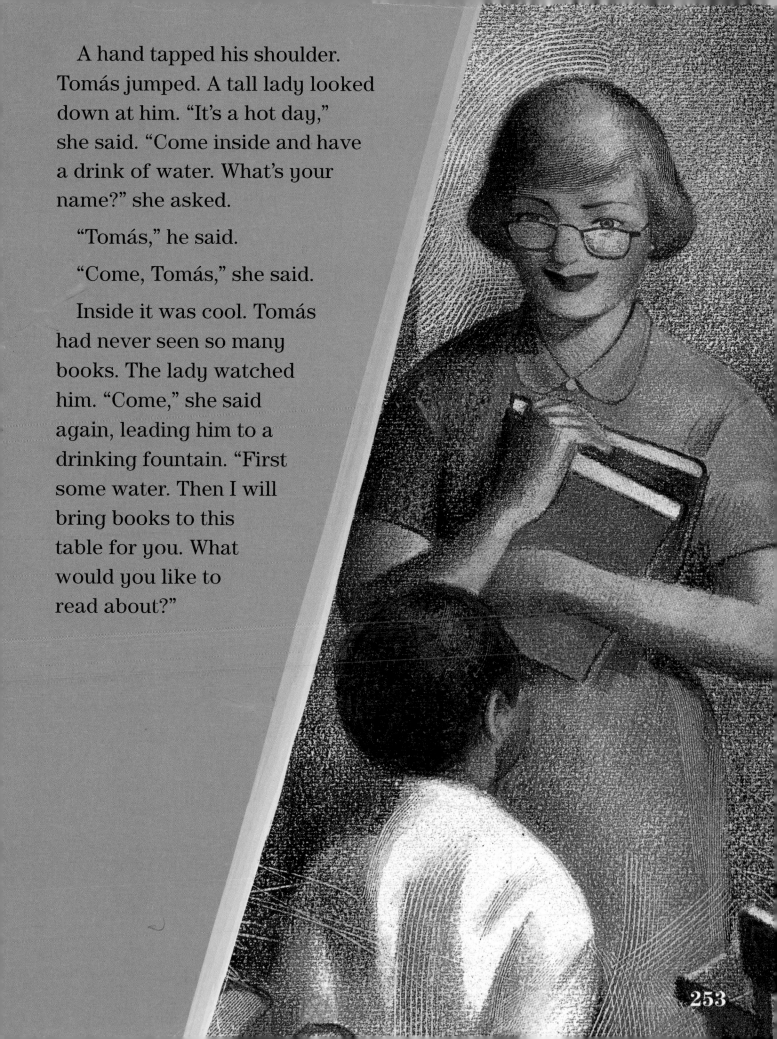

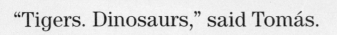

"Tigers. Dinosaurs," said Tomás.

Tomás drank the cold water. He looked at the tall
ceiling. He looked at all the books around the room.
He watched the lady take some books from the
shelves and bring them to the table. "This chair is for
you, Tomás," she said. Tomás sat down. Then very
carefully he took a book from the pile and opened it.

Tomás saw dinosaurs bending their long necks
to lap shiny water. He heard the cries of a wild
snakebird. He felt the warm neck of the dinosaur as
he held on tight for a ride. Tomás forgot about the
library lady. He forgot about Iowa and Texas.

"Tomás, Tomás," said the library lady softly. Tomás looked around. The library was empty. The sun was setting.

The library lady looked at Tomás for a long time. She said, "Tomás, would you like to borrow two library books? I will check them out in my name."

Tomás walked out of the library carrying his books. He ran home, eager to show the new stories to his family.

Papá Grande looked at the library books. "Read to me," he said to Tomás. First Tomás showed him the pictures. He pointed to the tiger. *"¡Que tigre tan grande!"* Tomás said first in Spanish and then in English, "What a big tiger!"

"Read to me in English," said Papá Grande. Tomás read about tiger eyes shining brightly in the jungle at night. He roared like a huge tiger. Papá, Mamá, and Enrique laughed. They came and sat near him to hear his story.

Some days Tomás went with his parents to the town dump. They looked for pieces of iron to sell. Enrique looked for toys. Tomás looked for books. He would put the books in the sun to bake away the smell.

All summer, whenever he could, Tomás went to the library. The library lady would say, "First a drink of water and then some new books, Tomás."

On quiet days the library lady said, "Come to my desk and read to me, Tomás." Then she would say, "Please teach me some new words in Spanish."

Tomás would smile. He liked being the teacher. The library lady pointed to a book. "Book is *libro*," said Tomás.

"*Libro*," said the library lady.

"*Pájaro*," said Tomás, flapping his arms.

The library lady laughed. "Bird," she said.

On days when the library was busy, Tomás read to himself. He'd look at the pictures for a long time. He smelled the smoke at an Indian camp. He rode a black horse across a hot, dusty desert. And in the evenings he would read the stories to Mamá, Papá, Papá Grande, and Enrique.

One August afternoon Tomás brought Papá
Grande to the library.

The library lady said, *"Buenas tardes, señor."*
Tomás smiled. He had taught the library lady how
to say "Good afternoon, sir" in Spanish.

"Buenas tardes, señora," Papá Grande replied.

Softly Tomás said, "I have a sad word to teach
you today. The word is *adiós*. It means good-bye."

Tomás was going back to Texas. He would miss
this quiet place, the cool water, the many books.
He would miss the library lady.

"My mother sent this to thank you," said Tomás, handing her a small package. "It is *pan dulce*, sweet bread. My mother makes the best *pan dulce* in Texas."

The library lady said, "How nice. How very nice. *Gracias*, Tomás. Thank you." She gave Tomás a big hug.

That night, bumping along again in the tired old car, Tomás held a shiny new book, a present from the library lady. Papá Grande smiled and said, "More stories for the new storyteller."

Tomás closed his eyes. He saw the dinosaurs drinking cool water long ago. He heard the cry of the wild snakebird. He felt the warm neck of the dinosaur as he held on tight for a bumpy ride.

Meet the Author

Pat Mora

Pat Mora started writing poems in elementary school, but she did not consider becoming an author until much later. Mora has now written over 25 books for children and 8 books for adults. She writes about what she likes and loves exploring new words and ideas. Mora also likes spending time with family and friends, gardening, and traveling.

Meet the Illustrator

Raul Colón

Raul Colón has illustrated magazine pages, theater posters, and advertisements, as well as, children's books. He has won many awards, including both Silver and Gold medals from the Society of Illustrators. In 2004, Colón published his first book as an author—*Orson Blasts Off.* He has lived in Puerto Rico and Florida, and now lives in New York.

Theme Connections

Within the Selection

1. How did you feel the first time you borrowed books from a library?

2. What kind of stories do you like to read?

Beyond the Selection

3. How do you use your imagination when you read or listen to a story?

4. How does a storyteller help you use your imagination?

Write about It!

Retell a story that a family member has told you.

Remember to write down names of your favorite books to add to the **Concept/ Question Board.**

Letter to the Senator

Dear Senator Woods:

I am writing to ask for your help. Soon you will vote on a bill that means a lot to my family. I refer to the Farm Bill; I hope that you will vote in favor of it.

We live on a fruit farm in the southern part of the state. We are proud of the organic produce that we grow and sell. It is an honor to provide these goods to our community.

Last fall I had the chance to join you at a town hall meeting. I was glad to hear you speak about the need to conserve farmland. The Farm Bill will encourage just that. It will reward farmers who keep their land productive and healthy. It will also provide funds for new ranchers and farmers.

Many farmers have suffered in times of drought. They have had to borrow money or sell their land. The Farm Bill would protect farmers from such drastic measures.

I know there are farms like ours across this country. I feel sure that the Farm Bill would benefit us all. I urge you to speak with Senators from other states and share your support for this bill.

I will be eager to learn the outcome of the vote. In the meantime, I trust that you will work with your colleagues to get this bill passed. Thank you for your service to our state and our nation.

Respectfully,

Kim Logan

Kim Logan

Think Link

1. What is the purpose of this business letter?

2. Why does the writer ask Senator Woods to speak with Senators from other states?

3. How is the salutation for a business letter different from that of a friendly letter?

Try It!

As you work on your investigation, think about how you should use colons when writing letters.

264

Read the story to find the meanings of these words, which are also in "Storm in the Night":

✦ mantel
✦ errand
✦ natural
✦ scarcely
✦ drenched
✦ siren
✦ overcome
✦ streaming

Vocabulary Strategy

Apposition is when a word or group of words define another word in the same sentence. Use apposition to find the meaning of *mantel*.

Vocabulary
Warm-Up

Pumpkin perched on the mantel, the shelf above the fireplace, where the cat preferred to sit. When a fire was lit, she could feel its warmth from below. From her post, Pumpkin also had a good view out the back window. She kept watch for intruders in the yard. No mouse was welcome.

After a nice nap, Pumpkin leaped down from her post. It was time to patrol the yard on foot. This was a daily errand that the cat enjoyed. After all, mice are a cat's natural enemy.

Pumpkin had scarcely begun her rounds when she sensed trouble. There was movement by the faucet at the back of the neighbor's house. A gap there in the concrete was inviting to mice. Now a mouse had come calling.

Pumpkin sprang into action. She pounced and swiped at the small rodent. The mouse slipped into the hole as Pumpkin's paw caught the faucet. All of a sudden, cold water sprayed and drenched the cat's face.

Pumpkin let out a yowl like a siren. She was brave when it came to mice, but Pumpkin had not overcome her fear of water. She jumped back and shook frantically.

At a safe distance from the faucet, Pumpkin thought about what to do next. There was no way to reach the mouse without getting even more wet. She would have to wait.

The cat headed back to the house. From behind the streaming water, a small pair of eyes watched Pumpkin retreat. The mouse had found a preferred spot of its own.

GAME

Making Sentences

Work with a partner to create sentences using the vocabulary words. Choose two words from the list, and challenge your partner to make up a sentence using the two words. Then switch roles. Continue until all of the vocabulary words have been used.

Concept Vocabulary

The concept vocabulary word for this lesson is **experiences. Experiences** are the events that a person has seen, done, or participated in. How does sharing experiences bring people together? What kinds of experiences are interesting to hear and read about?

Genre

Realistic Fiction involves stories about people and events that are true to life and that could really happen.

Comprehension Strategy

⭐ Summarizing
As you read, summarize what you have learned by rereading sections of the story or retelling the events in your own words.

STORM in the NIGHT

by **Mary Stolz**
illustrated by Pat Cummings

Focus Questions

How can listening to a story make you feel better when you are scared? How could hearing about stories of the past be important to you now and in the future?

Storm in the night.

Thunder like mountains blowing up.

Lightning licking the navy-blue sky.

Rain streaming down the windows, babbling in the downspouts.

And Grandfather? . . . And Thomas? . . . And Ringo, the cat?

They were in the dark.

Except for Ringo's shining mandarin eyes and the carrot-colored flames in the wood stove, they were quite in the dark.

"We can't read," said Grandfather.

"We can't look at TV," said Thomas.

"Too early to go to bed," said Grandfather.

Thomas sighed. "What will we do?"

"No help for it," said Grandfather, "I shall have to tell you a tale of when I was a boy."

Thomas smiled in the shadows.

It was not easy to believe that Grandfather had once been a boy, but Thomas believed it.

Because Grandfather said so, Thomas believed that long, long ago, probably at the beginning of the world, his grandfather had been a boy.

As Thomas was a boy now, and always would be.

A grandfather could be a boy, if he went back in his memory far enough; but a boy could not be a grandfather.

Ringo could not grow up to be a kangaroo, and a boy could not grow up to be an old man.

And that, said Thomas to himself, is that.

Grandfather was big and bearded.

Thomas had a chin as smooth as a peach.

Grandfather had a voice like a tuba.

Thomas's voice was like a penny whistle.

"I'm thinking," said Thomas.

"Ah," said Grandfather.

"I'm trying to think what you were like when you were my age."

"That's what I was like," said Grandfather.

"What?"

"Like someone your age."

"Did you look like me?"

"Very much like you."

"But you didn't have a beard."

"Not a sign of one."

"You were short, probably."

"Short, certainly."

"And your voice. It was like mine?"

"Exactly."

Thomas sighed. He just could not imagine it. He stopped trying.

He tried instead to decide whether to ask for a new story or an old one.

Grandfather knew more stories than a book full of stories.

Thomas hadn't heard all of them yet, because he kept asking for repeats.

As he thought about what to ask for, he listened to the sounds of the dark.

Grandfather listened too.

In the house a door creaked. A faucet leaked.

Ringo scratched on his post, then on Grandfather's chair.

He scratched behind his ear, and they could hear even that.

In the stove the flames made a fluttering noise.

"That's funny," said Thomas. "I can hear better in the dark than I can when the lights are on."

"No doubt because you are just listening," said his grandfather, "and not trying to see and hear at the same time."

That made sense to Thomas, and he went on listening for sounds in the dark.

There were the clocks.

The chiming clock on the mantel struck the hour of eight.

Ping, ping, ping, ping, ping, ping, ping, ping-a-ling.

The kitchen clock, very excited.

Ticktickticktickticktickety.

There were outside sounds for the listening, too.

The bells in the Congregational church rang through the rain.

Bong, bong, bong, bong, bong, bong, bong, BONG!

Automobile tires swished on the rain-wet streets.

Horns honked and hollered.

A siren whined in the distance.

"Grandfather," said Thomas, "were there automobiles when you were a boy?"

"Were there *automobiles*!" Grandfather shouted.

"How old do you think I am?"

"Well . . ." said Thomas.

"Next thing, you'll be asking if there was electricity when I was your age."

"Oh, Grandfather!" said Thomas, laughing.

After a while he said, "Was there?"

"Let's go out on the porch," said Grandfather.

"There's too much silliness in here."

By the light of the lightning they made their way to the front door and out on the porch.

Ringo, who always followed Thomas, followed him and jumped to the railing.

The rain, driving hard against the back of the house, was scarcely sprinkling here.

But it whooped windily through the great beech tree on the lawn, brandishing branches, tearing off twigs.

It drenched the bushes, splashed in the birdbath, clattered on the tin roof like a million tacks.

Grandfather and Thomas sat on the swing, creaking back and forth, back and forth, as thunder boomed and lightning stabbed across the sky.

Ringo's fur rose, and he turned his head from side to side, his eyes wide and wild in the flashes that lit up the night.

The air smelled peppery and gardeny and new.

"That's funny," said Thomas. "I can smell better in the dark, too."

Thomas thought Grandfather answered, but he couldn't hear, as just then a bolt of lightning cracked into the big beech tree. It ripped off a mighty bough, which crashed to the ground.

This was too much for Ringo. He leaped onto Thomas's lap and shivered there.

"Poor boy," said Thomas. "He's frightened."

"I had a dog when I was a boy," said Grandfather. "He was so scared of storms that I had to hide under the bed with him when one came. He was afraid even to be frightened alone."

"*I'm* not afraid of *anything,*" Thomas said, holding his cat close.

"Not many people can say that," said Grandfather. Then he added, "Well, I suppose anybody could say it."

"I'm not afraid of thunderstorms, like Ringo and your dog. What was his name?"

"Melvin."

"That's not a good name for a dog," Thomas said.

"I thought it was," Grandfather said calmly. "He was my dog."

"I like cats," said Thomas. "I want to own a *tiger*!"

"Not while you're living with me," said Grandfather.

"Okay," Thomas said. "Is there a story about Melvin?"

"There is. One very good one."

"Tell it," Thomas commanded. "Please, I mean."

"Well," said Grandfather, "when Melvin and I were pups together, I was just as afraid of storms as he was."

"No!" said Thomas.

"Yes," said Grandfather. "We can't all be brave as tigers."

"I guess not," Thomas agreed.

"So there we were, the two of us, hiding under beds whenever a storm came."

"Think of that . . ." said Thomas.

"That's what I'm doing," said Grandfather.

"Anyway, the day came when Melvin was out on some errand of his own, and I was doing my homework, when all at once, with only a rumble of warning . . .

down came the rain, *down* came the lightning, and all around and everywhere came the thunder."

"Wow," said Thomas. "What did you do?"

"Dove under the bed."

"But what about Melvin?"

"I'm *coming* to that," said Grandfather. "What-about-Melvin is what the story is *about.*"

"I see," said Thomas. "This is pretty exciting."

"Well—it was then. Are you going to listen, or keep interrupting?"

"I think I'll listen," said Thomas.

"Good. Where was I?"

"Under the bed."

"So I was. Well, I lay there shivering at every clap of thunder, and I'm ashamed to say that it was some time before I even remembered that my poor little dog was all by himself out in the storm."

Thomas shook his head in the dark.

"And when I did remember," Grandfather went on, "I had the most awful time making myself wriggle out from under the bed and go looking for my father or my mother—to ask them to go out and find Melvin for me."

"Grandfather!"

"I told you I was afraid. This is a true story you're hearing, so I have to tell the truth."

"Of course," said Thomas, admiring his grandfather for telling a truth like *that*. "Did you find them?"

"I did not. They had gone out someplace for an hour or so, but I'd forgotten. Thomas, fear does strange things to people . . . makes them forget everything but how afraid they are. You wouldn't know about that, of course."

Thomas stroked his cat and said nothing.

"In any case," Grandfather went on, "there I was, alone and afraid in the kitchen, and there was my poor little dog alone and afraid in the storm."

"What did you *do*?" Thomas demanded.

"You didn't *leave* him out there, did you, Grandfather?"

"Thomas—I put on my raincoat and opened the kitchen door and stepped out on the back porch just as a flash of lightning shook the whole sky and a clap of thunder barreled down and a huge man *appeared* out of the darkness, holding Melvin in his arms!"

"Whew!"

"That man was seven feet tall and had a face like a crack in the ice."

"Grandfather! You said you were telling me a true story."

"It's true, because that's how he looked to me. He stood there, scowling at me, and said, 'Son, is this your dog?' and I nodded, because I was too scared to speak. 'If you don't take better care of him, you shouldn't have him at all,' said the terrible man. He pushed Melvin at me and stormed off into the dark."

"Gee," said Thomas. "That wasn't very fair. He didn't know you were frightened too. I mean, Grandfather, how old were you?"

"Just about your age."

"Well, some people my age can get pretty frightened."

"Not you, of course."

Thomas said nothing.

"Later on," Grandfather continued, "I realized that man wasn't seven feet tall, or even terrible. He was worried about the puppy, so he didn't stop to think about me."

"Well, *I* think he should have."

"People don't always do what they should, Thomas."

"What's the end of the story?"

"Oh, just what you'd imagine," Grandfather said carelessly. "Having overcome my fear enough to forget myself and think about Melvin, I wasn't afraid of storms anymore."

"Oh, good," said Thomas.

For a while they were silent.

The storm was spent. There were only flickers of lightning, mutterings of thunder, and a little patter of rain.

"When are the lights going to come on?" Thomas asked.

"You know as much as I do," said Grandfather.

"Maybe they won't come on for hours," said Thomas. "Maybe they won't come on until *tomorrow*!"

"Maybe not."

"Maybe they'll *never* come on again, and what will we do then?"

"We'll think of something," said Grandfather.

"Grandfather?"

"Yes, Thomas?"

"What I think . . . I think that maybe if you hadn't been here, and Ringo hadn't been here, and I was all alone in the house and there was a storm and the lights went out and didn't come on again for a long time, like this . . . I think maybe *then* I would be a *little* bit afraid."

"Perfectly natural," said Grandfather.

Thomas sighed.

Grandfather yawned.

Ringo jumpcd to thc porch floor and walked daintily into the garden, shaking his legs.

After a while the lights came on.

They turned them off and went to bed.

Meet the Author

Mary Stolz

Mary Stolz loved reading and writing as a child. Stolz took a break from writing to spend time with her family, but later she began writing again to distract herself from a painful illness. Stolz got well and continued writing. She lives in Florida and enjoys reading, cooking, and watching baseball.

Meet the Illustrator

Pat Cummings

When she was growing up, Pat Cummings moved a lot. Her father's job in the army took their family to many states and countries. When living in Germany, she developed an interest in fantasy stories while climbing the stairs of castles. Today, Cummings loves illustrating fantasy and funny books. She lives in Brooklyn, New York, with her husband and her cat.

Storytelling
Theme Connections

Within the Selection

1. What sound words help bring the story "Storm in the Night" to life?
2. What are some situations when your family tells stories?

Across Selections

3. How is Thomas from "Storm in the Night" like Tomás from "Tomás and the Library Lady"?
4. How are the boys different?

Beyond the Selection

5. What mood do you expect to feel in a story that takes place during a dark, stormy night?
6. Why do many people like scary stories?

Write about It!

Describe a time when you were afraid.

Remember to bring photographs showing people enjoying a story together to add to the **Concept/Question Board.**

Science Inquiry

Element Experiment

For ages, people have tried to make sense of the world. They looked to their surroundings. There was earth, solid beneath their feet. There was wind in the air. There was fire, sparked by lightning or made by hand. And there was water, falling from the sky and filling the oceans.

To early folks, all matter was thought to be made of some mix of earth, wind, fire, and water. Today, we know there are about one hundred natural elements that make up all matter. However, earth, wind, fire, and water are not among them.

One of the basic elements is iron, a metal. Iron is used to make strong tools. It also helps keep our bodies strong and fit. That is why iron is added to some kinds of food. Try this test to look for iron that we eat.

Here is what you need:

- 1 cup of cereal, enriched with iron

		8B		
24	25	26	27	28
Cr	Mn	Fe	Co	Ni
51.996	54.938	55.847	58.933	58.693
42	43	44	45	46
Mo	Tc	Ru	Rh	Pd
95.94	[98]	101.07	102.905	106.42
74	75	76	77	78
W	Re	Os	Ir	Pt
183.84	186.207	190.23	192.217	195.078
106	107	108	109	110
Sg	Bh	Hs	Mt	Ds
[266]	[264]	[269]	[268]	[271]

- a one-gallon plastic bag
- a rolling pin
- a bowl
- 1 cup of water
- a sturdy magnet

Here is what to do:

1. Put the cereal in the bag. Seal the bag.

2. Use the rolling pin to crush the cereal. Make a fine powder.

3. Pour the powder and water into the bowl. Stir.

4. Move the magnet through the cereal.

Do you see tiny, dark specks on the magnet? Those are bits of iron!

Think Link

1. How has human understanding changed over time about the elements of matter?

2. What is the difference between the bulleted list and the numbered list?

3. Why is the order of steps important when explaining a process?

Try It!

As you work on your investigation, think about how you can use a list to organize your information.

Genre

Expository Text
a nonfiction that is
written to inform,
to explain, or to
persuade.

Comprehension
Skill

⭐ Drawing
Conclusions
As you read, look
for small pieces of
information that
allow you to draw
conclusions about a
character or event in
the selection. A
conclusion must be
supported by the text.

Focus Questions

If you were not able
to write a story using
words, how would you
go about telling your
story? What can you
learn about a culture
through its storytelling?

288

PUEBLO STORYTELLER

by Diane Hoyt-Goldsmith
photographs by Laurence Migdale

289

Read the article to find the meanings of these words, which are also in "Pueblo Storyteller":

✦ cylinder
✦ pure
✦ modeling
✦ concentrate
✦ ancestors
✦ traditions
✦ pueblo
✦ modern

Vocabulary Strategy

Context Clues are hints in the text. They help you find the meanings of words. Use context clues to find the meaning of *cylinder*.

Vocabulary

Warm-Up

In the Pacific Northwest, cedar trees grow tall and straight. They are treasured as a natural resource—and as a source of art. These are the trees that Northwest natives carve to make totem poles.

After the cedar tree is cut, its bark is stripped off. This leaves a cylinder of pure wood. The artist sculpts with saws, knives, and other sharp tools, modeling the figures in the poles. He needs to concentrate and work with care. Animal and human forms take shape. When the sculpting is complete, the artist paints the pole.

The figures that are carved depend on the purpose of the pole. Some totem poles tell about a clan. Strong, noble creatures serve as symbols for ancestors. Many poles boast bears, eagles, and ravens.

Some totem poles portray legends. These tales are part of a tribe's traditions. Some tribes did not have a written language. So they used totems to pass down their stories.

A third kind of totem marks a special event. It might honor the birth of a child or a hunter's success. It might pay tribute to a person who has died.

Totem poles are unique to tribes in the Northwest. They would not be found in a pueblo of the Southwest. They were not made by tribes in the Midwest or Southeast.

For a time, totem poles were scarce. Some decayed. Some were put in museums. Thankfully, modern artists revived the craft. Now the poles stand tall once more to tell their stories.

GAME

Synonyms

List the vocabulary words on a sheet of paper. Beside each word, write a synonym for that word. When you and a classmate are both finished, compare the synonyms you listed for each vocabulary word.

Concept Vocabulary

The concept word for this lesson is *history.* **History** includes events that happened in the past as well as stories about the events. Many people like to learn about the history of their family or their culture. Do you think it is important to share and pass on these kinds of stories?

Genre

Expository Text is nonfiction that is written to inform, to explain, or to persuade.

Comprehension Skill

 Drawing Conclusions

As you read, look for small pieces of information that allow you to draw conclusions about a character or event in the selection. A conclusion must be supported by the text.

Focus Questions

If you were not able to write a story using words, how would you go about telling your story? What can you learn about a culture through its storytelling?

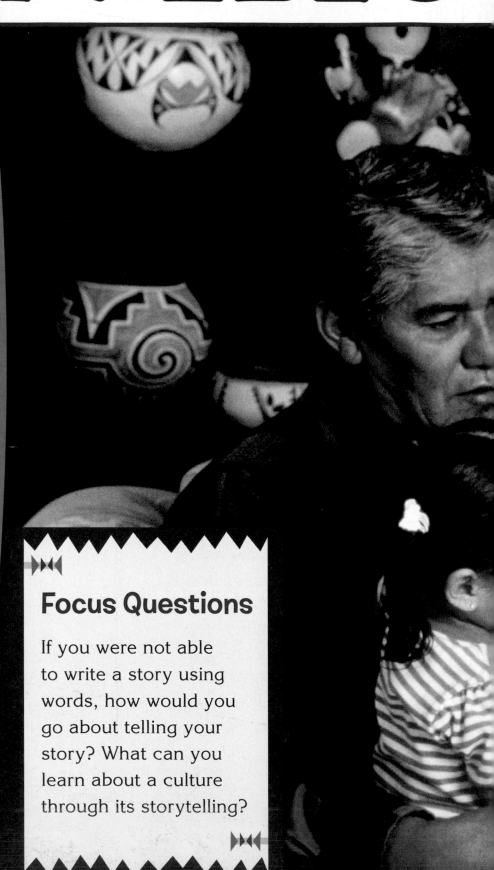

STORYTELLER

by Diane Hoyt-Goldsmith

photographs by Lawrence Migdale

April wears a handmade pueblo blouse and *manta*. The manta is a dress that covers one shoulder and is pinned on the side. Her jewelry was made by hand from silver and turquoise stones.

My name is April. I live with my grandparents in the Cochiti Pueblo near Santa Fe, New Mexico. Pueblo is a Spanish word that means "village" or "town." Our pueblo is very old. The Cochiti people have lived on these lands for many hundreds of years.

Although we live in the modern world, we like to stay close to nature, to the old ways and traditions. We learn about these traditions from our parents and grandparents.

My grandmother and grandfather make pottery in the traditional pueblo way. They do the work together. They do everything by hand. My grandmother learned to make pottery from her mother. Then she taught her daughters. Now she teaches me.

Making fine pottery has always been important to the pueblo people. The clay pots made by our ancestors were used for cooking, serving, and storing food. Sometimes pots were traded to other tribes. Today, there is at least one person in every Cochiti household who knows how to make pottery. Often pueblo families earn their living by selling the beautiful pots and figures that they make from the clay.

April helps her grandfather carry the clay back to the truck.

291

Each of the pueblos has its own place to get clay. The potters dig it from the ground. The clay comes in many natural colors. There are reds and browns and grays. There is even a pure white clay. Pueblo people make an offering of blue corn to thank the earth for providing the clay. Some families have gone to the same place to get the clay for generations.

My grandfather takes me with him when he goes for the clay. He drives to a faraway mesa where he can dig it from the ground. This is hard work!

The shadows are already long when April and her grandfather return to their pueblo with a load of clay. In the background are the Sandia Mountains.

Sometimes he has to crawl through a long tunnel of earth to find the clay. My grandfather uses a pick and a shovel to dig it out. We carry it back to our truck in buckets.

The clay is hard, like a rock. My grandfather soaks it in water until it becomes soft enough to work with his hands. He collects white sand from another place in the pueblo. He sifts the sand to remove the large rocks, sticks, and pebbles. Then he works the fine sand into the red clay to give it texture and make it stronger.

I like to watch my grandfather as he works. He kneads the clay together with the sand in the same way that my grandmother and I knead the dough for our bread. He works the clay with his hands until it feels just right.

When the clay is ready, my grandmother takes it and shows me how to begin. First we make a flat piece called a slab, and then we curve it to form a cylinder. This shape becomes the body of the clay figure my grandmother teaches me to make. It is the figure of a Pueblo Storyteller.

April's grandfather kneads the fine sand into the clay indoors, where the wind will not blow it away.

April's grandmother shows her how to join the edges of the slab with a little water to form a cylinder.

Since the early days of pueblo life, our people have learned about the past by listening to storytellers. Until now, we have never had a written language, so many of our stories cannot be found in books. This is why the storyteller is such an important person in our culture. This is also why so many potters in the Cochiti Pueblo make clay figures of the storyteller.

When my grandmother makes a Storyteller, she always thinks about her own grandfather. When she was a young girl, she enjoyed many happy hours in his company. In those days, they didn't have a television or a gas heater. She would sit on her grandfather's lap near a little fireplace in the corner of the room and listen to him tell stories about his life.

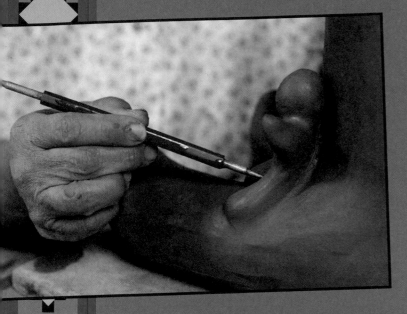

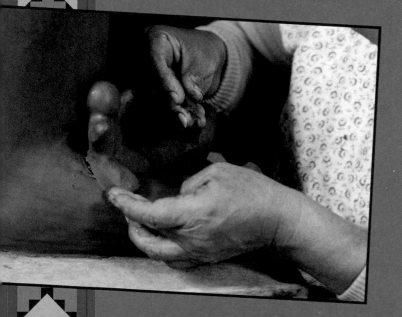

April's grandmother makes the figure of a little child. Then she attaches the child to the body of the Storyteller with bits of moistened clay.

Working on the clay figure, my grandmother creates a face that looks like her grandfather's. She gives him the traditional hairstyle of a pueblo man from the old days. She models the clay to show his long hair pulled back in a loop behind his head with a colorful band to hold it in place.

My grandmother makes arms and legs from smaller cylinders. She attaches these to the body with bits of moistened clay. Then she models boots or moccasins from the clay.

She always makes his face look very kind. He sits with his mouth open, as if he were singing a song or telling a story. His eyes are closed as he thinks in the backward way, remembering the past.

A Storyteller is left to dry in the corner of the kitchen. On the shelf above the clay figure, you can see a ladle made from a gourd.

Each potter who makes a Storyteller figure works in a different style. Some Storytellers are large and some are small. Many potters create the figure of a woman, remembering a favorite aunt or grandmother. Others, like my grandmother, design a figure that reminds them of their grandfather.

When the Storyteller is complete, my grandmother makes many tiny figures out of the clay. These are shaped like little pueblo children and she attaches them, one by one, to the Storyteller figure. She crowds them all onto his lap, so they can listen carefully to his tales, just as she did long ago.

April's grandfather shows her how to sand a Storyteller. Sanding makes the surface smooth enough to paint.

My grandmother adds as many children as she can fit. She tells me that on every Storyteller she makes, there is one child who looks just like me! This makes me feel very special.

After all the modeling is finished, the pottery is left to dry. This takes many days.

When the pottery is hard and dry, it is my grandfather's turn to work on it. He rubs the surfaces of the pottery with sandpaper until they are smooth enough to paint. My grandfather tells me he likes to be in a happy, patient mood when he is sanding the pottery. The work must be done carefully. It cannot be rushed.

Sometimes the pottery will break or crack before it is finished. Instead of throwing the ruined pottery away in the garbage, the pueblo potters give the clay back to the earth where it came from. My grandfather often takes a broken pot down to the river and throws it in the water. Sometimes he will take the broken pieces back up into the hills near the pueblo.

After the pieces are sanded, my grandmother covers them with a thin layer of white clay that has been mixed with water, called slip. When the slip dries, it gives the pottery a clean, white surface that can be polished and painted.

To get a shiny surface, my grandmother polishes her pots with special stones. These polishing stones are very important to the pueblo potters. Each one gives a different patina or shine. Polishing stones are treasured, and the good ones are passed down from one generation to the next.

My grandmother likes to paint her pottery in a very quiet place. She needs to concentrate so that the lines she draws will be straight and the shapes that she makes will be beautiful.

For the red color, my grandmother uses a clay that is mixed with water. For the black, she uses guaco, an inky liquid made by boiling down a wild plant that grows in the fields near our house. It is called Rocky Mountain beeweed. This same plant is something we pick in the spring and eat as one of our vegetables.

After my grandmother finishes painting the pottery, it is time for the firing. This is the final step. Firing the pottery makes the clay very strong so it will last for a long time.

My grandparents work together to build a kiln outside in the yard. They go out to the pasture and collect many pieces of dried cow manure. We call these "cow pies" because

they are so flat and round. My grandparents lay some wood under a metal grate and put the pottery on top of it. They arrange the cow pies in a single layer on the top and sides of the pottery.

The cow pies are mostly made of grass, and they burn easily. They make the fire all around the pottery burn evenly at a very high temperature. We burn cow pies instead of wood because they do not contain pitch or sap that could stain the beautifully painted surfaces of the pottery.

After the fire is lit, we can only watch and wait. When the fire burns out and the pottery cools, my grandmother rakes the ashes away. We carefully remove the pottery and clean off any small bits of grit or ash. "Now the work is finished," my grandfather tells me proudly. "It is perfect and beautiful, made by our own hands from the earth's elements of fire, water, and clay."

Meet the Author

Diane Hoyt-Goldsmith

Diane Hoyt-Goldsmith writes and designs books. "I love writing nonfiction because I enjoy learning about the world we live in," Hoyt-Goldsmith says. "I like to meet new people and learn about their lives." She is fascinated by the art of the Northwest Coast Indian tribes, which she used as motivation for her first book, *Totem Pole*.

Meet the Photographer

Lawrence Migdale

Lawrence Migdale was born in Johannesburg, South Africa. As a young man, he bought his first camera and traveled to Europe and Israel. Migdale now works as a freelance photographer and focuses on topics for children's books.

Storytelling

Theme Connections

Within the Selection

1. How would it feel to be a village storyteller?
2. If you made a Storyteller figure, who would you model it after?

Across Selections

3. What does April from "Pueblo Storyteller" have in common with Thomas from "Storm in the Night"?
4. Suppose archaeologists like those in "Days of Digging" uncovered Storyteller figures hundreds of years from now. What could they learn about the Cochiti culture from the clay figures?

Beyond the Selection

5. What are some traits of a good storyteller?
6. What are some features of a good story?

Write about It!

Describe the differences between stories that are written and stories that are passed on orally.

Remember to write the name of your favorite author or storyteller to add to the **Concept/Question Board**.

The Quechan Culture

An outline is a great planning tool for writers. It lists the main ideas of a report. It also shows important details the writer will include. Here is one student's outline for a report about the Quechan people.

Outline for Report on Quechan Indian Tribe

I. The Quechan lived along the Colorado River.
   A. The land they settled is now part of Arizona and California.
   B. Spring floods made the land good for farming.

II. The Quechan farmed, hunted, and gathered food.
   A. They planted corn, beans, and squash in the rich river silt.
   B. They hunted rabbits and birds and caught fish.
   C. They gathered the pods of mesquite trees and other wild plants.

III. The Quechan built shelters from natural materials.
   A. Houses were built from cottonwood, arrowweed, and earth.

B. Ramadas, or sun shades, were made of branches and brush.

IV. The Quechan made clothes from plants and animals.

   A. Women wore skirts made from strips of willow bark.

   B. In cold weather, they used cloaks and blankets made of rabbit fur.

   C. Sandals were made from plant fibers.

V. The Quechan made crafts and tools from clay.

   A. They dug clay from the hillsides and ground.

   B. Hand-modeled clay dolls are one of the Quechan craft traditions.

   C. Clay pots were used to cook, serve, and store food.

Think Link

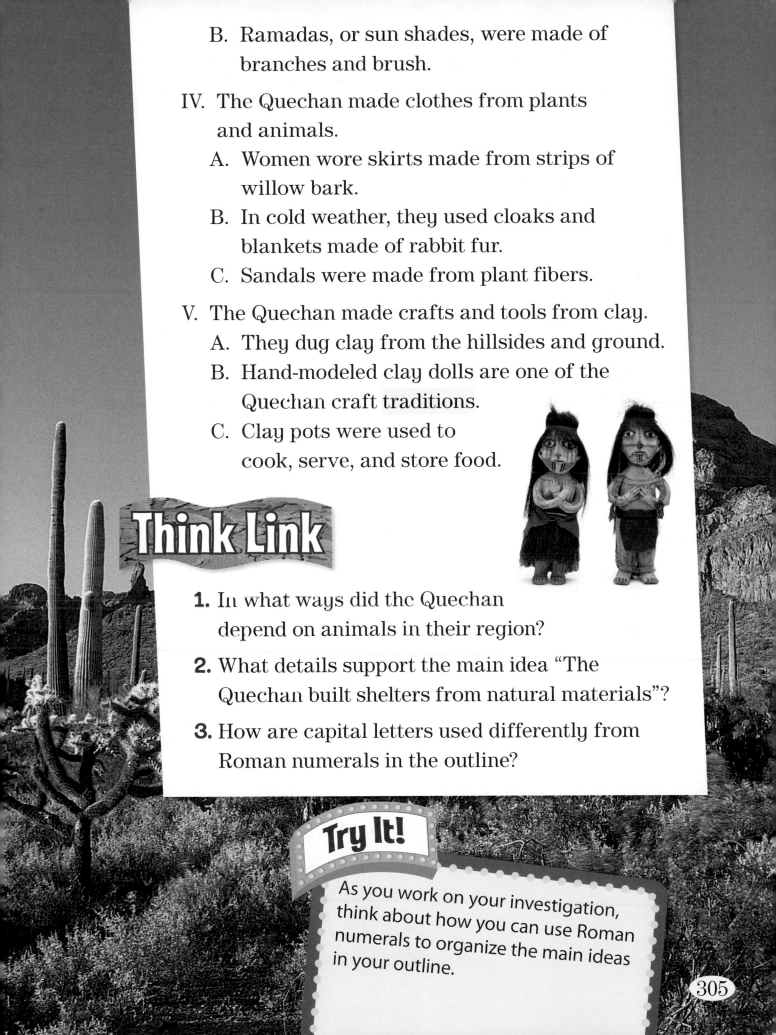

1. In what ways did the Quechan depend on animals in their region?

2. What details support the main idea "The Quechan built shelters from natural materials"?

3. How are capital letters used differently from Roman numerals in the outline?

Try It!

As you work on your investigation, think about how you can use Roman numerals to organize the main ideas in your outline.

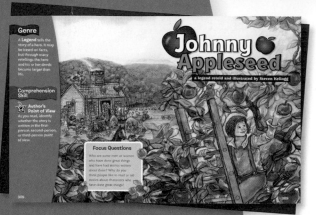

Read the story to find the meanings of these words, which are also in "Johnny Appleseed":

- ✦ cleared
- ✦ stored
- ✦ boasted
- ✦ exaggerated
- ✦ exhausted
- ✦ affectionately
- ✦ claim
- ✦ survived

Vocabulary Strategy

Word Structure is when parts of a word help you understand the word's meaning. Use word structure to find the meaning of *affectionately*.

Vocabulary

Warm-Up

All of us kids loved Aunt Lou. Her real name was Louise, but we called her Aunt Lou. Oh, and she was not really our aunt. She was our neighbor.

Aunt Lou's house was the best one on the block. Any summer afternoon, you were certain to find kids there. Every morning she cleared her wide front porch of any chairs and put out big plastic bins. She stored treasures for us within these bins.

Some bins held sticky jugs of liquid for blowing bubbles. There were also chunks of sidewalk chalk and tattered jump ropes. Bats, balls, and hula hoops were always on hand.

There was a set of bowling pins and a bowling ball that we used on the porch. Aunt Lou boasted about being a champion bowler, but she never won a game. Maybe she exaggerated about her skill. Or maybe she just let us win.

By the time we left Aunt Lou's each day, we were exhausted. Aunt Lou, however, was not. She would set to work in her garden. Aunt Lou talked affectionately to her plants. Some people claim Aunt Lou's flowers survived a late frost because she talked them through it!

It has been ten years since I last saw Aunt Lou. I figured I should call and say hello. When Aunt Lou answered the phone, I asked if she recalled me and the other kids. "Oh, yes, dear," she said. "But can I call you back? It's my turn at bat!"

GAME

Crossword Puzzle

Create a crossword puzzle with the vocabulary words. Figure out how you will have the words overlap, and draw empty boxes for the letters. Create separate sets of clues for words that go "Across" and words that go "Down." Give your puzzle to a classmate to complete.

Concept Vocabulary

The concept vocabulary word for this lesson is **chronicle.** A **chronicle** is a written record of events. Can you think of a type of chronicle you have read or written? What is the value of a chronicle? Discuss your ideas with classmates.

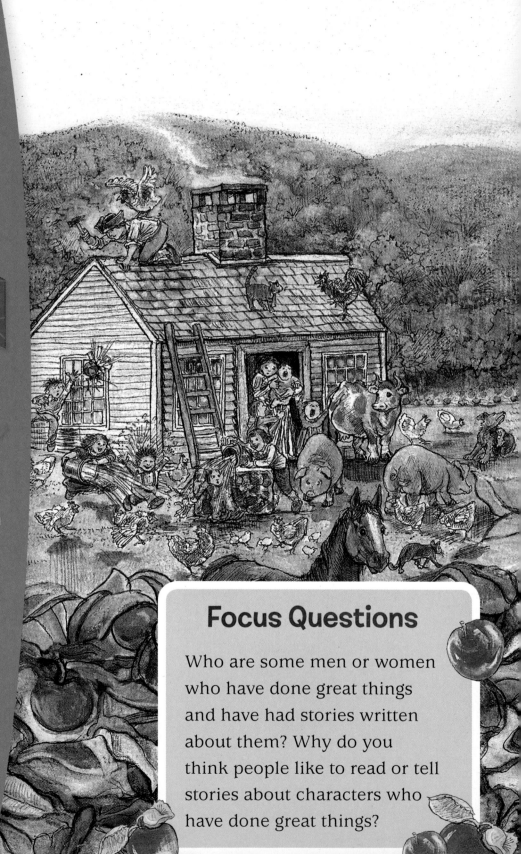

Focus Questions

Who are some men or women who have done great things and have had stories written about them? Why do you think people like to read or tell stories about characters who have done great things?

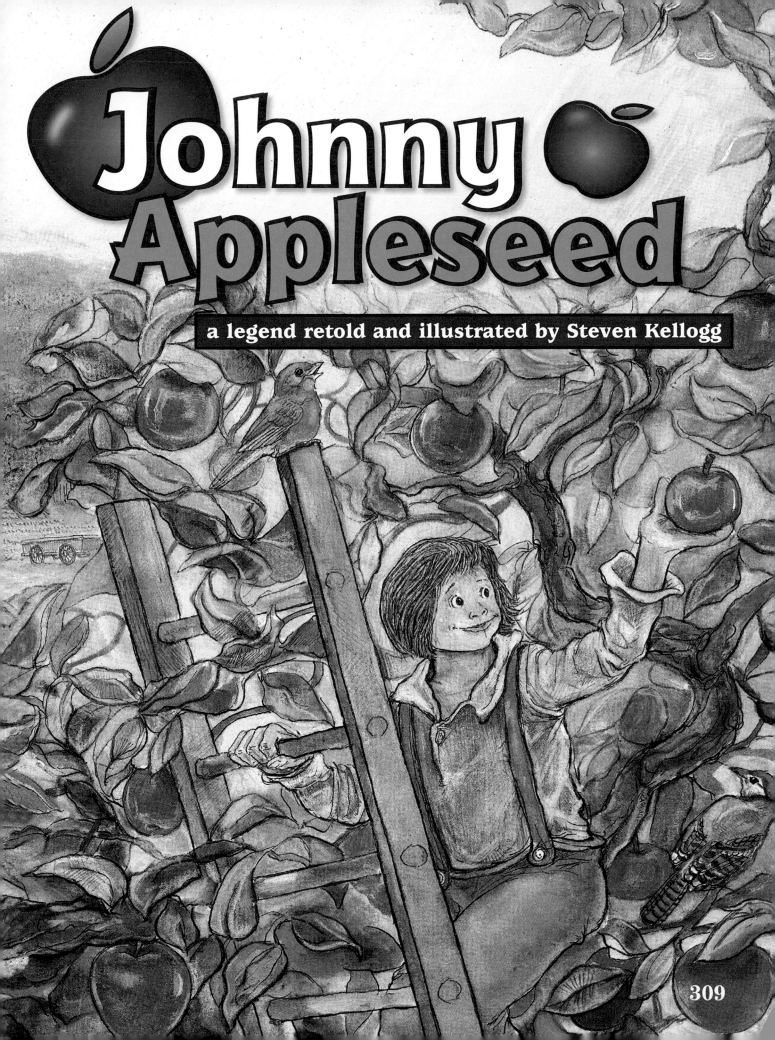

Johnny Appleseed

a legend retold and illustrated by Steven Kellogg

John Chapman, who later became known as Johnny Appleseed, was born on September 26, 1774, when the apples on the trees surrounding his home in Leominster, Massachusetts, were as red as the autumn leaves.

John's first years were hard. His father left the family to fight in the Revolutionary War, and his mother and his baby brother both died before his second birthday.

By the time John turned six, his father had remarried and settled in Longmeadow, Massachusetts. Within a decade their little house was overflowing with ten more children.

Nearby was an apple orchard. Like most early American families, the Chapmans picked their apples in the fall, stored them in the cellar for winter eating, and used them to make sauces, cider, vinegar, and apple butter. John loved to watch the spring blossoms slowly turn into the glowing fruit of autumn.

Watching the apples grow inspired in John a love of all of nature. He often escaped from his boisterous household to the tranquil woods. The animals sensed his gentleness and trusted him.

As soon as John was old enough to leave home, he set out to explore the vast wilderness to the west. When he reached the Allegheny Mountains, he cleared a plot of land and planted a small orchard with the pouch of apple seeds he had carried with him.

John walked hundreds of miles through the Pennsylvania forest, living like the Indians he befriended on the trail. As he traveled, he cleared the land for many more orchards. He was sure the pioneer families would be arriving before long, and he looked forward to supplying them with apple trees.

When a storm struck, he found shelter in a hollow log or built a lean-to. On clear nights he stretched out under the stars.

Over the next few years, John continued to visit and care for his new orchards. The winters slowed him down, but he survived happily on a diet of butternuts.

One spring he met a band of men who boasted that they could lick their weight in wildcats. They were amazed to hear that John wouldn't hurt an animal.

They challenged John to compete at wrestling, the favorite frontier sport. He suggested a more practical contest—a tree-chopping match. The woodsmen eagerly agreed.

When the sawdust settled, there was no question about who had come out on top. John was pleased that the land for his largest orchard had been so quickly cleared. He thanked the exhausted woodsmen for their help and began planting.

During the next few years, John continued to move westward. Whenever he ran out of apple seeds, he hiked to the eastern cider presses to replenish his supply. Before long, John's plantings were spread across the state of Ohio.

Meanwhile, pioneer families were arriving in search of homesites and farmland. John had located his orchards on the routes he thought they'd be traveling. As he had hoped, the settlers were eager to buy his young trees.

John went out of his way to lend a helping hand to his new neighbors. Often he would give his trees away. People affectionately called him Johnny Appleseed, and he began using that name.

He particularly enjoyed entertaining children with tales of his wilderness adventures and stories.

In 1812 the British incited the Indians to join them in another war against the Americans. The settlers feared that Ohio would be invaded from Lake Erie.

It grieved Johnny that his friends were fighting each other. But when he saw the smoke of burning cabins, he ran through the night, shouting a warning at every door.

After the war, people urged Johnny to build a house and settle down. He replied that he lived like a king in his wilderness home, and he returned to the forest he loved.

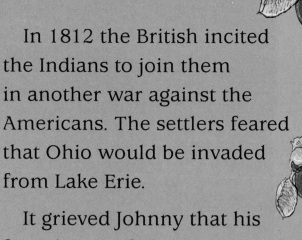

During his long absences, folks enjoyed sharing their recollections of Johnny. They retold his stories and sometimes they even exaggerated them a bit.

Some recalled Johnny sleeping in a treetop hammock and chatting with the birds.

Others remembered that a rattlesnake had attacked his foot. Fortunately, Johnny's feet were as tough as elephant's hide, so the fangs didn't penetrate.

It was said that Johnny had once tended a wounded wolf and then kept him for a pet.

An old hunter swore he'd seen Johnny frolicking with a bear family.

The storytellers outdid each other with tall tales about his feats of survival in the untamed wilderness.

As the years passed, Ohio became too crowded for Johnny. He moved to the wilds of Indiana, where he continued to clear land for his orchards.

When the settlers began arriving, Johnny recognized some of the children who had listened to his stories. Now they had children of their own.

It made Johnny's old heart glad when they welcomed him as a beloved friend and asked to hear his tales again.

When Johnny passed seventy, it became difficult for him to keep up with his work. Then, in March of 1845, while trudging through a snowstorm near Fort Wayne, Indiana, he became ill for the first time in his life.

Johnny asked for shelter in a settler's cabin, and a few days later he died there.

Curiously, Johnny's stories continued to move westward without him. Folks maintained that they'd seen him in Illinois or that he'd greeted them in Missouri, Arkansas, or Texas. Others were certain that he'd planted trees on the slopes of the Rocky Mountains or in California's distant valleys.

Even today people still claim they've seen
Johnny Appleseed.

Meet the Author and Illustrator

Steven Kellogg

Steven Kellogg was in preschool when he decided to become an artist. He used to play a game called "Telling Stories on Paper" with his sisters. The game involved Kellogg making up stories and drawing pictures to go with them. Kellogg lives in an old farmhouse in Connecticut with his wife, six stepchildren, and a lot of dogs and cats. He loves animals, and his pets have become characters in many of his books.

Theme Connections

Within the Selection

1. What other famous people in American history have you read stories about?

2. Which of your hobbies or talents would be featured in a legend about you?

Across Selections

3. How were the storytellers in "Johnny Appleseed" like the Cochita people in "Pueblo Storyteller"?

4. Do you think the clay Storyteller figure would be a fitting symbol for Johnny Appleseed? Explain.

Beyond the Selection

5. How is telling a story different from reading a story aloud?

6. Which kind of storytelling do you like better?

Write about It!

Describe an adventure you have had.

Remember to record questions about legends and other types of folktales to add to the **Concept/Question Board**.

321

The Pomo Is a Fact-Filled Account

Suzanne Freedman's book *The Pomo* paints a clear picture of these Native Americans. The Pomo were some of the first people to make their home in California. Their story goes back thousands of years. That is where Freedman begins.

At first, the Pomo were seven distinct tribes. Still, these groups had a lot in common. Life was much the same in each Pomo village. They had the same type of homes. Boys were taught to hunt and fish. Girls learned to cook food and make baskets.

A wealth of details about Pomo culture are found in the book. Freedman covers topics such as art, beliefs, food, clothes, and games. Drawings and photos help bring the text to life. They show tools and crafts used and made by the Pomo.

The author writes about less pleasant subjects too. She tells how settlers changed the Pomo way of life. The tribe was on good terms with early Russian traders, but in time, other settlers would abuse them. Pomo were forced to work as slaves. Their land was stolen.

The tribe dwindled, but it was not destroyed. Those who survived the hard times kept up their customs. To this day, thousands of Pomo live in California. Most make their homes near Clear Lake. Many of them still speak the Pomo language. They still eat native foods. They still weave baskets.

The Pomo is not a source for current data on the tribe. However, it is filled with rich details of the past. Those who research the tribe are certain to find this book worthwhile.

Think Link

1. Why is it important to set a book's title apart from the rest of the text? In which two paragraphs of this review is the book's title given?

2. How are book reviews helpful to readers?

3. What was the writer's opinion of this book? Support your answer with details from the review.

Try It!

As you work on your investigation, remember to use italic type when referring to the title of a book.

Read the story to find the meanings of these words, which are also in "McBroom and the Big Wind":

+ common
+ huddled
+ haste
+ calculate
+ gust
+ deny
+ battered
+ shingle

Vocabulary Strategy

Context Clues are hints in the text. They help you find the meanings of words. Use context clues to find the meaning of *shingle*.

Vocabulary
Warm-Up

It was a common spring morning. Cole was running late—again. When his mom told him to get up, he had said, "Later." When she told him to eat his eggs, Cole said, "Later."

Now Mom called out, "Cole, put your umbrella in your backpack."

"Later," said Cole, as he jammed a toothbrush in his mouth. He smiled at himself in the mirror, then bounded down the stairs. Cole grabbed his coat and backpack. "See ya, Mom!" he yelled.

As he stepped out the door, Cole heard a great rumble. A mass of dark clouds huddled over the neighborhood. In his haste to get ready, Cole had

not heard the approaching storm. He had also forgotten to pack his umbrella.

The rain came in a burst, and Cole bolted for the bus shelter. Water pooled in potholes. Cole came to a large puddle and tried to calculate the distance across. He figured he could make it, but a great gust of wind blew him back. Cole landed with a splash.

At last, Cole reached the bus shelter. He could not deny that he was grateful for the weathered old hut. Cole stepped inside and let out a sigh of relief. He was surprised to find that raindrops still battered his head.

Then Cole saw the ragged gaps in the roof, and he remembered. Last month, Cole's dad had come to him. He had said he needed to shingle the roof of the old shelter again, and he wanted Cole to help. Cole had said, "Sure, Dad. Later."

GAME

Charades

Use the vocabulary words to play a game of charades with classmates. Choose one of the words to act out. The first person to correctly identify the word *and* explain its meaning gets to take the next turn as actor.

Concept Vocabulary

The concept word for this lesson is *humor.* **Humor** is a quality that makes something funny. Folktales, and other kinds of stories, often include humor. Talk about the use of humor in this story. Why do you think humor is an element of many popular stories?

Genre

A Tall Tale
uses humorous exaggeration to tell about situations that would not happen in real life. A tall tale is also about a fictional character who often solves problems in creative ways.

Comprehension Skill

 Compare and Contrast
As you read, compare and contrast familiar ideas or things with ideas or things that are unfamiliar.

McBroom

Focus Questions

What emotions have you experienced when reading or hearing stories? How might you use storytelling to get others to feel certain feelings? To tell others about yourself?

and the Big Wind

by Sid Fleischman

illustrated by Mark A. Hicks

I can't deny it—it does get a mite windy out here on the prairie. Why, just last year a blow came ripping across our farm and carried off a pail of sweet milk. The next day it came back for the cow.

But that wasn't the howlin', scowlin', almighty *big* wind I aim to tell you about. That was just a common little prairie breeze. No account, really. Hardly worth bragging about.

It was the *big* wind that broke my leg. I don't expect you to believe that—yet. I'd best start with some smaller weather and work up to that bonebreaker.

I remember distinctly the first prairie wind that came scampering along after we bought our wonderful one-acre farm. My, that land is rich. Best topsoil in the country. There isn't a thing that won't grow in our rich topsoil, and fast as lightning.

The morning I'm talking about our oldest boys
were helping me to shingle the roof. I had bought
a keg of nails, but it turned out those nails were a
whit short. We buried them in our wonderful topsoil
and watered them down. In five or ten minutes
those nails grew a full half-inch.

So there we were, up on the roof, hammering
down shingles. There wasn't a cloud in the sky at
first. The younger boys were shooting marbles all
over the farm and the girls were jumping rope.

When I had pounded down the last shingle I said
to myself, "Josh McBroom, that's a mighty stout
roof. It'll last a hundred years."

Just then I felt a small draft on the back of my
neck. A moment later one of the girls—it was Polly,
as I recall—shouted up to me. "Pa," she said, "do
jackrabbits have wings?"

I laughed. "No, Polly."

"Then how come there's a flock of jackrabbits
flying over the house?"

I looked up. Mercy! Rabbits were flapping their ears across the sky in a perfect V formation, northbound. I knew then we were in for a slight blow.

"Run, everybody!" I shouted to the young'uns. I didn't want the wind picking them up by the ears. "Will*jill*hester*chester*peter*polly*tim*tom*mary*larry*-andlittle*clarinda*—in the house! Scamper!"

The clothesline was already beginning to whip around like a jump rope. My dear wife, Melissa, who had been baking a heap of biscuits, threw open the door. In we dashed and not a moment too soon. The wind was snapping at our heels like a pack of wolves. It aimed to barge right in and make itself at home! A prairie wind has no manners at all.

We slammed the door in its teeth. Now, the wind didn't take that politely. It rammed and battered at the door while all of us pushed and shoved to hold the door shut. My, it was a battle! How the house creaked and trembled!

"Push, my lambs!" I yelled. "Shove!"

At times the door planks bent like barrel staves. But we held that roaring wind out. When it saw there was no getting past us, the zephyr sneaked around the house to the back door. However, our oldest boy, Will, was too smart for it. He piled Mama's heap of fresh biscuits against the back door. My dear wife, Melissa, is a wonderful cook, but her biscuits *are* terribly heavy. They made a splendid door stop.

But what worried me most was our wondrous rich topsoil. That thieving wind was apt to make off with it, leaving us with a trifling hole in the ground.

"Shove, my lambs!" I said. "Push!"

The battle raged on for an hour. Finally the wind gave up butting its fool head against the door. With a great angry sigh it turned and whisked itself away, scattering fence pickets as it went.

We all took a deep breath and I opened the door a crack. Hardly a leaf now stirred on the ground. A bird began to twitter. I rushed outside to our poor one-acre farm.

331

Mercy! What I saw left me popeyed. "Melissa!" I shouted with glee. "Will*jill*hester*chester*peter*polly*tim*tom*mary*larry*andlittle*clarinda*! Come here, my lambs! Look!"

We all gazed in wonder. Our topsoil was still there—every bit. Bless those youngsters! The boys had left their marbles all over the field, and the marbles had grown as large as boulders. There they sat, huge agates and sparkling glassies, holding down our precious topsoil.

But that rambunctious wind didn't leave empty-handed. It ripped off our new shingle roof. Pulled out the nails, too. We found out later the wind had shingled every gopher hole in the next county.

Now that was a strong draft. But it wasn't a *big* wind. Nothing like the kind that broke my leg. Still, that prairie gust was an education to me.

"Young'uns," I said, after we'd rolled those giant marbles down the hill. "The next uninvited breeze that comes along, we'll be ready for it. There are two sides to every flapjack. It appears to me the wind can be downright useful on our farm if we let it know who's boss."

The next gusty day that came along, we put it to work for us. I made a wind plow. I rigged a bedsheet and tackle to our old farm plow. Soon as a breeze sprung up I'd go tacking to and fro over the farm, plowing as I went. Our son Chester once plowed the entire farm in under three minutes.

On Thanksgiving morning Mama told the girls to pluck a large turkey for dinner. They didn't much like that chore, but a prairie gust arrived just in time. The girls stuck the turkey out the window. The wind plucked that turkey clean, pinfeathers and all.

Oh, we got downright glad to see a blow come along. The young'uns were always wanting to go out and play in the wind, but Mama was afraid they'd be carried off. So I made them wind shoes— made 'em out of heavy iron skillets. Out in the breeze those shoes felt light as feathers. The girls would jump rope with the clothesline. The wind spun the rope, of course.

Many a time I saw the youngsters put on their wind shoes and go clumping outside with a big tin funnel and all the empty bottles and jugs they could round up. They'd cork the containers jam full of prairie wind.

Then, come summer, when there wasn't a breath of air, they'd uncork a bottle or two of fresh winter wind and enjoy the cool breeze.

Of course, we had to windproof the farm every fall. We'd plant the field in buttercups. My, they were slippery—all that butter, I guess. The wind would slip and slide over the farm without being able to get a purchase on the topsoil. By then the boys and I had reshingled the roof. We used screws instead of nails.

Mercy! Then came the *big* wind!

It started out gently enough. There were a few jackrabbits and some crows flying backward through the air. Nothing out of the ordinary.

Of course the girls went outside to jump the clothesline and the boys got busy laying up bottles of wind for summer. Mama had just baked a batch of fresh biscuits. My, they did smell good! I ate a dozen or so hot out of the oven. And that turned out to be a terrible mistake.

Outside, the wind was picking up ground speed and scattering fence posts as it went.

"Will*jill*hester*chester*peter*polly*tim*tom*mary*larry*-and little *clarinda*!" I shouted. "Inside, my lambs! That wind is getting ornery!"

The young'uns came trooping in and pulled off their wind shoes. And not a moment too soon. The clothesline began to whip around so fast it seemed to disappear. Then we saw a hen house come flying through the air, with the hens still in it.

The sky was turning dark and mean. The wind came out of the far north, howling and shrieking and shaking the house. In the cupboard, cups chattered in their saucers.

Soon we noticed big balls of fur rolling along the prairie like tumbleweeds. Turned out they were timber wolves from up north. And then an old hollow log came spinning across the farm and split against my chopping stump. Out rolled a black bear, and was he in a temper! He had been trying to hibernate and didn't take kindly to being awakened. He gave out a roar and looked around for somebody to chase. He saw us at the windows and decided we would do.

The mere sight of him scared the young'uns and they huddled together, holding hands, near the fireplace.

I got down my shotgun and opened a window. That was a *mistake!* Two things happened at once. The bear was coming on and in my haste I forgot to calculate the direction of the wind. It came shrieking along the side of the house and when I poked the gunbarrel out the window, well, the wind bent it like an angle iron. That buckshot flew due south. I found out later it brought down a brace of ducks over Mexico.

But worse than that, when I threw open the window such a draft came in that our young'uns *were sucked up through the chimney!* Holding hands, they were carried away like a string of sausages.

Mama near fainted away. "My dear Melissa," I exclaimed. "Don't you worry! I'll get our young'uns back!"

I fetched a rope and rushed outside. I could see the young'uns up in the sky and blowing south.

I could also see the bear and he could see me. He gave a growl with a mouthful of teeth like rusty nails. He rose up on his hind legs and came toward me with his eyes glowing red as fire.

I didn't fancy tangling with that monster. I dodged around behind the clothesline. I kept one eye on the bear and the other on the young'uns. They were now flying over the county seat and looked hardly bigger than mayflies.

The bear charged toward me. The wind was spinning the clothesline so fast he couldn't see it. And he charged smack into it. My, didn't he begin to jump! He jumped red-hot pepper, only faster. He had got himself trapped inside the rope and couldn't jump out.

Of course, I didn't lose a moment. I began flapping my arms like a bird. That was such an enormous *big* wind I figured I could fly after the young'uns. The wind tugged and pulled at me, but it couldn't lift me an inch off the ground.

Tarnation! I had eaten too many biscuits. They were heavy as lead and weighed me down.

The young'uns were almost out of sight. I rushed to the barn for the wind plow. Once out in the breeze, the bedsheet filled with wind. Off I shot like a cannonball, plowing a deep furrow as I went.

Didn't I streak along, though! I was making better time than the young'uns. I kept my hands on the plow handles and steered around barns and farmhouses. I saw haystacks explode in the wind. If that wind got any stronger it wouldn't surprise me to see the sun blown off course. It would set in the south at high noon.

I plowed right along and gained rapidly on the young'uns. They were still holding hands and just clearing the tree tops. Before long I was within hailing distance.

"Be brave, my lambs!" I shouted. "Hold tight!"

I spurted after them until their shadows lay across my path. But the bedsheet was so swelled out with wind that I couldn't stop the plow. Before I could let go of the handles and jump off I had sailed far *ahead* of the young'uns.

I heaved the rope into the air. "Will*jill*hester*chester*-peter*polly*tim*tom*mary*larry*andlittle*clarinda*!" I shouted as they came flying overhead. "Hang on!"

Hester missed the rope, and Jill missed the rope, and so did Peter. But Will caught it. I had to dig my heels in the earth to hold them. And then I started back. The young'uns were too light for the wind. They hung in the air. I had to drag them home on the rope like balloons on a string.

Of course it took most of the day to shoulder my way back through the wind. It was a mighty struggle, I tell you! It was near suppertime when we saw our farmhouse ahead, and that black bear was still jumping rope!

I dragged the young'uns into the house. The rascals! They had had a jolly time flying through the air, and wanted to do it again! Mama put them to bed with their wind shoes on.

The wind blew all night, and the next morning that bear was still jumping rope. His tongue was hanging out and he had lost so much weight he was skin and bones.

Finally, about midmorning, the wind got tired of blowing one way, so it blew the other. We got to feeling sorry for that bear and cut him loose. He was so tuckered out he didn't even growl. He just pointed himself toward the tall timber to find another hollow log to crawl into. But he had lost the fine art of walking. We watched him jump, jump, jump north until he was out of sight.

That was the howlin', scowlin' all mighty *big* wind that broke my leg. It had not only pulled up fence posts, but the *holes* as well. It dropped one of those holes right outside the barn door and I stepped in it.

That's the bottom truth. Everyone on the prairie knows Josh McBroom would rather break his leg than tell a fib.

Meet the Author

Sid Fleischman

Sid Fleischman saw a magician when he was in fifth grade, and he decided he wanted to be one too. He became a pretty good magician. He never planned to be a writer, but after writing for a newspaper, Fleischman found that he loved telling stories. He has written about 60 books, some of which have been made into movies. Fleischman lives in California and loves the sound of the ocean.

Meet the Illustrator

Mark Hicks

Mark Hicks has illustrated many children's books. He also owns a 90-pound Sulcata tortoise, who lives in his yard and keeps the grass mowed by eating it. Besides being an illustrator, Hicks is also an inventor who loves collecting antique books and toys.

Theme Connections

Within the Selection

1. What clues tell you whether a story is true or completely made up?

2. How does the author make the wind into a character in this story?

Across Selections

3. How is "McBroom and the Big Wind" similar to "Johnny Appleseed"?

4. How are the stories different?

Beyond the Selection

5. What are some ways writers create humor in a story?

6. How does dialogue add to a story?

Write about It!

Use exaggeration to describe a time when you have "battled" nature.

Remember to bring in examples of other tall tales to add to the **Concept/Question Board**.

Energy Forecast: Sunny and Windy

Energy comes from many sources. Most of the energy we use comes from fossil fuels. These include coal, oil, and gas. We also use other sources of energy, like the sun and wind. This is important because fossil fuels cannot be renewed. When they are gone, we cannot make more.

Solar (from the sun) and wind energies can be renewed. Each day there is sun and wind. Both can also be changed to electric power, used by people all over the world.

The sun and wind are also good power sources because they are clean. When we burn coal and oil, it pollutes the air. Energy we get from the sun and wind does not harm the air.

The sun and wind are renewable, clean—and free! So, why not use these sources more? The main reason is consistency.

The sun and wind are not always present in the same amounts. On cloudy days and at night, the sun cannot be used. Also, no place has a constant gust of wind. Solar energy can be stored in batteries and used later. Unfortunately, wind cannot be stored.

Cost is a problem too. Setting up wind or solar power plants is very expensive. In addition, these kinds of power plants take up a lot of land.

Still, no one can deny the value of solar and wind power. The world's energy needs grow each day, but our fossil fuel supply is shrinking. That is why the sun and the wind are sure to play a big role in our future.

Think Link

1. Why are solar and wind energies considered "clean"?

2. Why is the use of solar and wind energies likely to increase in the future?

3. How do the words in parentheses help the reader?

Try It!

As you work on your investigation, be sure to use parentheses around information you would like to add in a sentence.

Aunt Sue's Stories

by Langston Hughes

illustrated by
Shelley Johnson

Aunt Sue has a head full of stories.
Aunt Sue has a whole heart full of stories.
Summer nights on the front porch
Aunt Sue cuddles a brown-faced child to her bosom
And tells him stories.

Black slaves
Working in the hot sun,
And black slaves
Walking in the dewy night,
And black slaves
Singing sorrow songs on the banks of a mighty river
Mingle themselves softly
In the flow of old Aunt Sue's voice,
Mingle themselves softly
In the dark shadows that cross and recross
Aunt Sue's stories.

And the dark-faced child, listening,
Knows that Aunt Sue's stories are real stories.
He knows that Aunt Sue never got her stories
Out of any book at all,
But that they came
Right out of her own life.

And the dark-faced child is quiet
Of a summer night
Listening to Aunt Sue's stories.

Focus Questions How can old pictures tell stories?
How can you learn about your family's past
by looking at old photographs?

Ode to Family Photographs

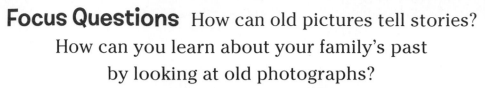

by Gary Soto
illustrated by Dom Lee

This is the pond, and these are my feet.
This is the rooster, and this is more of my feet.

Mamá was never good at pictures.

This is a statue of a famous general who
lost an arm,
And this is me with my head cut off.

This is a trash can chained to a gate,
This is my father with his eyes half-closed.

This is a photograph of my sister
And a giraffe looking over her shoulder.

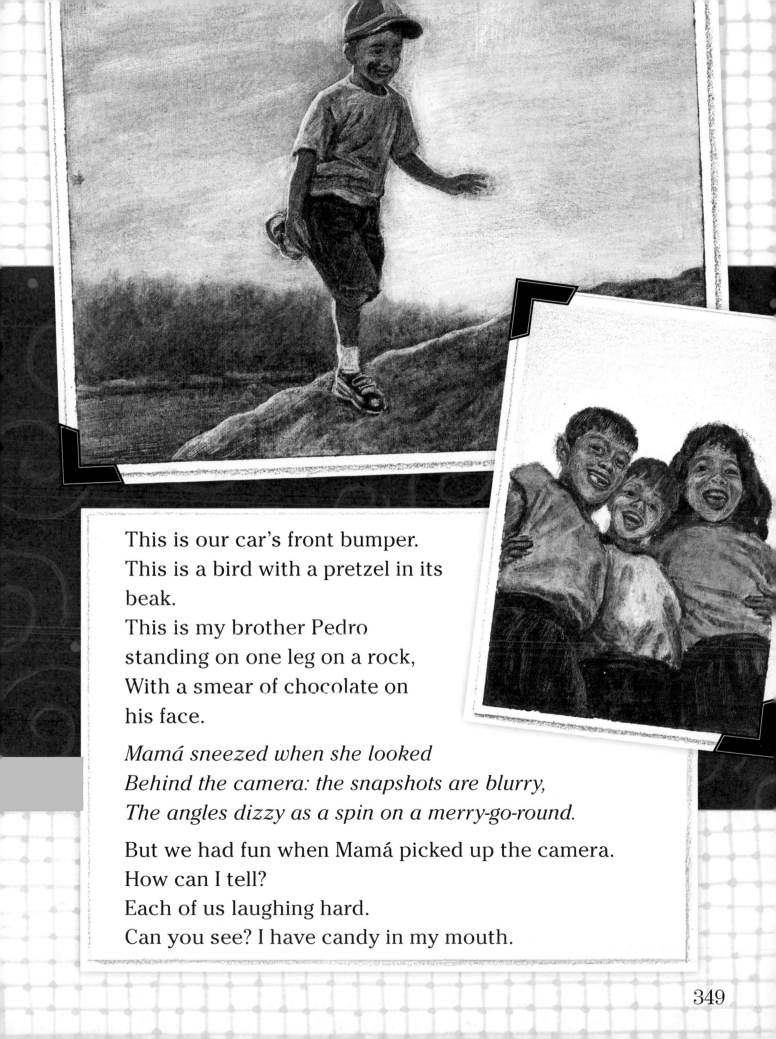

This is our car's front bumper.
This is a bird with a pretzel in its
beak.
This is my brother Pedro
standing on one leg on a rock,
With a smear of chocolate on
his face.

Mamá sneezed when she looked
Behind the camera: the snapshots are blurry,
The angles dizzy as a spin on a merry-go-round.

But we had fun when Mamá picked up the camera.
How can I tell?
Each of us laughing hard.
Can you see? I have candy in my mouth.

Test-Taking Strategy: Taking the Best Guess When Unsure of the Answer

Sometimes you will not know which answer is correct. When this happens, take your best guess.

Taking the Best Guess When Unsure of the Answer

Sometimes you might not know the answer on a test. When this happens, take your best guess. When you guess, you will be correct some of the time.

Try not to guess too often. It is always better to think about the question, look at the answer choices, and choose the one you think is correct.

> **Read the sentences. Look at the answers. Think about the answer that means the same as *vacant*.**
>
> The trail was vacant. All the other hikers had gone home.
> Ⓐ beautiful   Ⓑ narrow
> Ⓒ empty   Ⓓ blocked

How do you know which answer is correct? Think about the second sentence. It says, "All the other hikers had gone home." The sentence helps you know that *empty* is the correct answer.

The information in the sentence helps you find the answer. If you still cannot figure it out, take your best guess.

Test-Taking Practice

Read the story "Family Tall Tales." Then answer numbers 1 through 4.

Every year we have a family reunion at the lake. We like to have fun at our reunions. This year we decided that we would tell stories.

Uncle Leroy would be the storytelling leader. He said that everyone had to exaggerate or brag. Doing this would make the stories more fun. He had another good idea. The person who told the best tall tale would get a prize. He did not say what the prize was. He wanted us to be surprised.

After lunch, we sat down on the grass. We formed a big circle so that we could see each other. Each one of us took a turn telling our stories.

Mom began with her story. She said, "I caught a fish that was five feet long." We knew she caught only a little trout.

My sister bragged, "I was chosen to be in the Miss Florida beauty pageant." My brother laughed and said she was in a school fashion show.

GO ON

Uncle Leroy stretched the truth and said, "I swam a mile to rescue a dog from a flash flood." We knew that it was not a flood. Street drains near his house got stopped up. A dog was playing in the water and wanted Uncle Leroy to play.

My cousin, Sue, told about the time she found an alligator in her backyard. We heard that a little lizard had crawled onto her chair and scared her.

Uncle Pat was sure that his story would win. He said, "We had snow in Florida. It got so deep that all you could see were the tops of palm trees." Aunt Dot smiled and added, "Well, it wasn't actually snow. It was not even near our house. At the north end of Florida, they had some frost."

We told stories until it got dark. It was a lot of fun, and we laughed a lot. Uncle Leroy was glad that everyone told a good story. Then it was time to choose a winner. Uncle Leroy stood up to announce the winner. He said that everyone told such good stories that we would all get a prize. He gave us shirts that said "Best Family Tall Tale."

GO ON

Use what you learned from "Family Tall Tales" to answer Numbers 1 through 4. Write your answers on a piece of paper.

Test Tips

- Say the question to yourself.

- Look at each answer.

- Skip difficult items and come back to them later.

1. In this story, the word *reunion* means a kind of

Ⓐ job.

Ⓑ party.

Ⓒ contest.

Ⓓ picture.

2. What gives Uncle Leroy the idea for his story about swimming in a flood?

Ⓐ Catching a fish five feet long

Ⓑ Watching his family at the lake

Ⓒ Playing with a dog in the water

Ⓓ Seeing snow up to the tops of trees

3. What happens just after Uncle Pat tells his story?

Ⓐ Aunt Dot explains that his story is made up.

Ⓑ The family decides to have a storytelling contest.

Ⓒ Everyone sits in a circle so they can see Uncle Pat.

Ⓓ Uncle Leroy gives him a prize for telling stories.

4. How are all the family stories alike?

Ⓐ They are all long and complicated.

Ⓑ They are all about animals.

Ⓒ They are all about weather.

Ⓓ They are all tall tales.

Pronunciation Key

a as in **at**
ā as in **late**
â as in **care**
ä as in **father**
e as in **set**
ē as in **me**
i as in **it**
ī as in **kite**
o as in **ox**
ō as in **rose**

ô as in **bought** and **raw**
oi as in **coin**
ōō as in **book**
ōō as in **too**
or as in **form**
ou as in **out**
u as in **up**
ū as in **use**
ûr as in **turn**, **germ**, **learn**, **firm**, **work**

ə as in **about**, **chicken**, **pencil**, **cannon**, **circus**
ch as in **chair**
hw as in **which**
ng as in **ring**
sh as in **shop**
th as in **thin**
t͡h as in **there**
zh as in **treasure**

The mark (ˊ) is placed after a syllable with a heavy accent, as in **chicken** (**chik**ˊ ən).

The mark (ˏ) after a syllable shows a lighter accent, as in **disappear** (**dis**ˊ əp **pēr**ˊ).

Glossary

A

acres (ā´ kûrz) *n.* Plural form of **acre:** A measurement equal to 43,560 square feet.

adjust (əd just´) *v.* To change for the purpose of correcting something.

admire (əd mīr´) *v.* To look at with pleasure.

affectionately (əf fek´ shən ət lē) *adv.* With love.

aftershocks (af´ tûr shoks´) *n.* Plural form of **aftershock:** A vibration of rocks or plates shifting into a new position.

alarm (əl ärm´) *n.* A sudden fear of danger.

ambitions (am bish´ ənz) *n.* Plural form of **ambition:** A strong desire to do or succeed at something.

ancestors (an´ ses tûrz´) *n.* Plural form of **ancestor:** An older family member from long ago.

arrowhead (âr´ rō hed) *n.* The tip of an arrow.

artifacts (är´ ti fakts´) *n.* Plural form of **artifact:** An old tool, a weapon, or other thing made by people in the past.

astronaut (as´ tro not´) *n.* A person who is trained to pilot or be a part of the crew of a spacecraft.

Astronomers (as tron´ əm ûrz´) *n.* Plural form of **astronomer:** Someone who studies stars.

astronomy (as tron´ əm ē´) *n.* The study of objects in space.

atmosphere (at´ məs fēr´) *n.* Area of gas surrounding a planet.

aurora (ə ror´ ə) *n.* The appearance of light in the night sky.

axis (ak´ sis) *n.* A real or an imaginary straight line through the center of an object, around which the object turns.

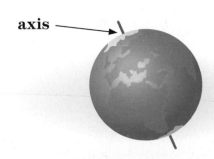

axis →

Pronunciation Key: at; lāte; câre; fäther; set; mē; it; kīte; ox; rōse; ô in bought; coin; book; too; form; out; up; ūse; tûrn; ə sound in about, chicken, pencil, cannon, circus; chair; hw in which; ring; shop; thin; there; zh in treasure.

B

bald (bôld) *adj.* Without hair on the head.

battered (bat´ tûrd) *v.* Past tense of **batter:** To hit over and over again with heavy blows.

beats (bēts) *v.* A form of the verb **beat:** To come down strong and continuously.

boasted (bōst´ əd) *v.* Past tense of **boast:** To brag.

boiled (boil d) *v.* Past tense of **boil:** To heat until steaming.

bolt (bōlt) *n.* A lightning streak.

borrow (bor´ rōw) *v.* To take something from another person with the understanding that it must be given back.

bough (bou) *n.* A tree branch.

bow (bou) *n.* The front part of a boat.

brandishing (bran´ dish ing) *v.* Form of **brandish:** to shake threateningly.

brave (brāv) *adj.* Not afraid; showing courage.

broil (broil) *v.* To make very hot.

burrows (bûr´ rowz) *n.* Plural form of **burrow:** A hole in the ground where some animals live.

burrows

burst (bûrst) *v.* To break open suddenly.

bursts (bûrsts) *n.* Plural form of **burst:** An explosion.

bushy (boosh´ ē) *adj.* Shaggy and thick.

C

calculate (kal´ kū lāt´) *n.* To figure out.

carpenters (kär´ pən dûrz´) *n.* Plural form of **carpenter:** A person who builds and repairs houses and other things made of wood.

century (sen´ chə rē) n. A period of one hundred years.

certain (sûr´ tən) adj. Sure.

challenge (chal´ lənj) v. To give the best of.

chant (chant) v. To sing words over and over.

charted (chärt´ əd) v. A form of the verb **chart**: To map; to show information as a picture.

chronicle (kron´ ik əl) n. A written record of events.

clay (klā) n. Soft sticky mud.

claim (klām) v. 1) To take as one's own. 2) To say that something is true.

clap (klap) n. A loud sound.

cleared (klērd) v. Past tense of **clear**: To remove things from.

clerk (klûrk) n. A person who sells goods or services to customers.

commander (kəm mand´ ûr) n. The captain leading a ship or voyage.

common (kom´ mən) adj. Happening often; familiar.

community (kəm mū´ ni tē) n. A group of people who live in the same area or have a shared interest.

concentrate (kon´ sən trāt) v. To give careful attention.

constellation (kon´ stəl lā´ shən) n. A related group of stars.

contain (kən tān´) v. To hold.

cot (kot) n. A type of bed.

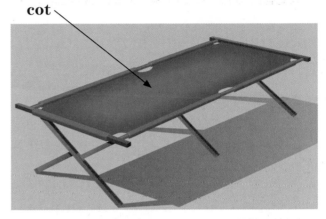

cot

crackled (krak´ əl d) v. Past tense of **crackle**: To make a snapping noise.

creative (krē āt´ əv´) adj. Able to make or invent new things.

crescent moon (kres´ ənt mo͞on´) n. The curved shape of the waxing or waning moon.

crops (krops) n. Plural form of **crop**: Plants grown to be used as food or sold for profit.

crumbling (krum´ bəl ing) v. A form of the verb **crumble**: To fall to pieces.

Pronunciation Key: at; lāte; câre; fäther; set; mē; it; kīte; ox; rōse; ô in bought; coin; bŏŏk; tōō; form; out; up; ūse; tûrn; ə sound in about, chicken, pencil, cannon, circus; chair; hw in which; ring; shop; thin; there; zh in treasure.

cultures (kəl´ chûrz) *n.* Plural form of **culture:** The arts, beliefs, and customs that make up a way of life for a group of people at a certain time.

curve (kûrv) *n.* A bending line.

customs (kus´ təmz) *n.* Plural form of **custom:** A practice that has become accepted by many people; a tradition.

cycle (sī´ kəl) *n.* A series of events that happens regularly.

cylinder (sil´ in dûr) *n.* A solid or hollow object shaped like a drum or a soup can.

D

damaged (dam´ ijd) *v.* Past tense of **damage:** To make something less valuable or useful.

den (den) *n.* A place where wild animals rest or sleep.

deny (də nī´) *v.* To say that something is not true.

desolation (des´ ə lā´ shən) *n.* Emptiness.

developed (də vel´ əpd) *v.* Past tense of **develop:** To grow; to change.

development (də vel´ əp mənt´) *n.* Growth or change.

devices (də vīs´ əz) *n.* Plural form of **device:** A machine.

directions (də rek´ shənz) *n.* Plural form of **direction:** The way to get somewhere.

discount (dis´ kount) *adj.* With lowered prices.

downtown (doun´ toun) *n.* The main part or business district of a town.

draft (draft) *n.* A current of air in a room.

drenched (drenchd) *v.* Past tense of **drench:** To soak completely.

drenched

dump (dump) *n.* A place where garbage and trash are thrown.

E

eager (ē′ gûr) *adj.* Wanting very much to do something.

earthquake (ûrth′ kwāk) *n.* A shaking or trembling of the ground.

elevated (el′ əv āt′ əd) *adj.* Raised above the ground.

engineers (en′ jən ērz′) *n.* Plural form of **engineer:** A person trained to plan and design things such as bridges, roads, or airplanes.

eroding (ə rōd′ ing) *n.* The process of wearing or washing away slowly.

errand (er′ rənd) *n.* A short trip to do something.

exactly (eg zakt′ lē) *adv.* Without any mistakes.

exaggerated (egz aj′ jûr āt′ əd) *v.* Past tense of **exaggerate:** To go beyond the truth.

excavation (eks′ ka vā′ shən) *n.* A site created by digging. The process of creating the site.

exhausted (egz ôst′ əd) *adj.* Very weak or tired.

experiences (eks pē′ rē əns′ əz) *n.* Plural form of **experience:** The event that a person has seen, done, or participated in.

expire (eks pīr′) *v.* To come to an end.

F

faucet (fô′ sət) *n.* A water tap.

featuring (fē′ chûr ing) *adj.* Having as the main attraction.

fierce (fērs) *adj.* Strong and wild; raging.

filters (fil′ tûrz) *n.* Plural form of **filter:** A device or material used to block certain light rays.

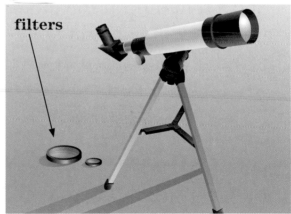

filters

finally (fī′ nəl lē) *adv.* At last.

flickers (flik′ ûrz) *n.* Plural form of **flicker:** A short burst of light.

Pronunciation Key: at; lāte; câre; fäther; set; mē; it; kīte; ox; rōse; ô in bought; coin; bŏŏk; tōō; form; out; up; ūse; tûrn; ə sound in about, chicken, pencil, cannon, circus; chair; hw in which; ring; shop; thin; there; zh in treasure.

foam (fōm) *n.* A mass of bubbles.

foundation (foun dā´shən) *n.* The base upon which a structure is built.

frames (frāmz) *n.* Plural form of **frame:** The skeleton of a building.

full moon (fəl mōōn) *n.* Seeing the whole circle of the moon.

funnel (fun´nəl) *n.* A utensil with a wide cone at one end and a thin tube at the other, used to pour something into a container with a small opening without spilling.

G

gas (gas) *n.* Heating or cooking fuel.

gases (gas´əz) *n.* Plural form of **gas:** A form of matter that is not solid or liquid.

gathered (gath´ûrd) *v.* Past tense of **gather:** To collect.

gazed (gāzd) *v.* Past tense of **gaze:** To stare.

generations (jen´ûr ā´shənz) *n.* Plural form of **generation:** A period of about thirty years.

gigantic (jī gan´tik) *adj.* Very big.

gigantic

gravity (gra´və tē´) *n.* The force pulling things toward the center of a body in space, such as Earth or the moon.

grieved (grēvd) *v.* Past tense of **grieve:** To mourn; to feel sad.

gulps (gulps) *n.* Plural form of **gulp:** A large amount swallowed at one time.

gust (gust) *n.* A sudden, strong rush of wind or air.

half (haf) *adj.* One of two equal parts.

haste (hāst) *n.* Quickness in moving or in acting; speed.

hibernate (hī´ bûr nāt) *v.* To sleep through the winter months.

history (his´ tûr ē) *n.* Events that happened in the past as well as stories about the events.

horizon (hə rī´ zən) *n.* The line where the sky and the land or sea seem to meet.

horizon

howling (houl´ ing) *v.* A form of the verb **howl:** To make a loud, wailing cry.

huddled (hud´ dəld) *v.* Past tense of **huddle:** To crowd together.

humor (hū´ mûr) *n.* A quality that makes something funny.

imagination (i maj´ ə nā´ shən) *n.* The ability to form mental images, or pictures.

inspired (in spīrd´) *v.* Past tense of **inspire:** To fill with a strong, encouraging feeling.

installed (in stôld´) *v.* A form of the verb **install:** To put in place for use or service.

invaded (in vād´ əd) *v.* Past tense of **invade:** To attack in order to conquer the land or people.

iron (ī´ ûrn) *n.* A gray-white metal used to make steel.

jumped (jumpd) *v.* Past tense of **jump:** To move or get up suddenly.

Pronunciation Key: at; lāte; câre; fäther; set; mē; it; kīte; ox; rōse; ô in bought; coin; book; too; form; out; up; ūse; tûrn; ə sound in about, chicken, pencil, cannon, circus; chair; hw in which; ring; shop; thin; there; zh in treasure.

K

kiln (kiln) *n.* A type of oven used for making bricks, pottery, and charcoal.

kiln

kneads (nēdz) *v.* A form of the verb **knead:** To mix and press together with the hands.

L

laboratory (la´ brə tor´ ē) *n.* A room for science experiments and tests.

lap (lap) *v.* To drink a liquid by lifting it up with the tongue.

layer (lā´ ûr) *n.* A single thickness of something.

lighted (līt´ əd) *adj.* That which is showing light.

M

magnetic field (mag ned´ik fēld´) *n.* The space around a magnet in which the magnet has the power to attract other metals.

mantel (man´ təl) *n.* A shelf above a fireplace.

mantel

mesa (mā´ sə) *n.* A hill or mountain with a flat top and steep sides.

missions (mish´ ənz) *n.* Plural form of **mission:** A special job or task given to a person or group.

modeling (mod´ əl ing) *n.* The making or designing of something.

modern (mod´ ûrn) *adj.* From the present or recent time.

mounted (mount´ əd) *v.* A form of the verb **mount:** To place or fix on to something.

natural (nach´ ûr əl) *adj.* Found in nature; not made by people.

necessities (nəs es´ sət ēz´) *n.* Plural form of **necessity:** Something that is needed.

new moon (noo moon´) *n.* The moon when it cannot be seen or when it appears as a thin crescent.

O

occur (ək kûr´) *v.* To happen.

orbit (or´ bit) *n.* The path in space that an object follows as it moves in a circle around a planet, moon, or star. *v.* To circle around a heavenly body, such as Earth or the moon.

origins (or´ ə gənz) *n.* Plural form of **origin:** The cause or source of something; what something begins as or comes from.

oval (ov´ əl) *adj.* Egg-shaped.

overcome (ō vûr cum´) *v.* To beat or conquer.

P

package (pak´ əj) *n.* A thing or group of things packed, wrapped up, or tied together; a bundle.

partial (pär´ shəl) *adj.* Part of; incomplete.

particular (pär´ tik´ ū lûr) *adj.* Special.

patches (pach´ əz) *n.* Plural form of **patch:** An area different than what is around it.

path (path) *n.* The route along which something travels.

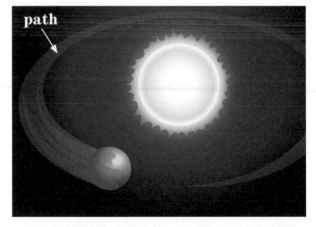

path

penetrate (pen´ ət rāt) *v.* To go into or pass through.

phases (fāz′ əz) *n.* Plural form of **phase:** The appearance and shape of the moon or a planet as it is seen at a particular time.

pile (pīl) *n.* A number of things lying one on top of the other; a heap.

pluck (pluk) *v.* To pull off; to pick.

power lines (pou′ ûr līnz) *n.* Plural form of **power line:** A wire that carries electricity.

practically (prak′ tik əl lē) *adv.* Almost.

precious (presh′ əs) *adj.* Of great value.

pressure (presh′ ûr) *n.* Weight of one thing pushing against another.

produce (prō′ doos) *n.* Farm products, such as fresh fruits and vegetables.

profitable (prof′ it ə bəl) *adj.* Moneymaking; rewarding.

property (prop′ ûr dē) *n.* Land that a person owns.

pueblo (poo e′ blō) *n.* A Native American village consisting of adobe and stone houses joined together.

pure (pūr) *adj.* Not mixed with anything else.

Q

quarantine (quor′ən tēn′) *n.* The keeping of a person, an animal, or a thing away from others to stop the spread of disease.

quarter moon (kwor′ tər moon′) *n.* Phase of the moon in which it looks like a half circle.

R

raged (rāj d) *v.* Past tense of **rage:** To storm violently.

rays (rāz) *n.* Plural form of **ray:** A beam of light or energy.

recalled (rē käld′) *v.* Past tense of **recall:** To remember.

recollections (rek əl lek´ shənz) *n*. Plural form of **recollection:** A memory.

relic (rel´ ik) *n*. Something that survives from an earlier time or place.

reluctantly (rə luk´ tənt lē´) *adv*. Not wanting to do something.

remained (rə mānd´) *v*. Past tense of **remain:** To stay.

research (rē sûrch´) *n*. A careful study to find and learn facts.

revolution (rev´ ə lōō´ shən) *n*. One time around a planet or star.

ringed (ringd) *adj*. Marked with a circular pattern.

ripples (rip´ pəlz) *n*. Plural form of **ripple:** A design created by waves.

ripples

rotation (rō tā´ shən) *n*. Motion about a center point, or an axis.

ruin (rōō´ in) *n*. Destruction, damage, or collapse.

rumble (rum´ bəl) *n*. A heavy, deep, rolling sound.

rusty (rust´ ē) *adj*. Covered with rust; the reddish brown or orange coating that forms on iron exposed to moisture or air.

scale (skāl) *n*. The size of a map, picture, or model compared with what it represents.

scarcely (skârs´ lē) *adv*. Barely.

scowling (skoul´ ing) *adj*. Frowning.

scraped (skrāpd) *v*. Past tense of **scrape:** To push or pull an object over another.

seasonal (sē´ zən əl) *adj*. Ripe at a certain time.

section (sek´ shən) *n*. A part of something.

Pronunciation Key: at; lāte; câre; fäther; set; mē; it; kīte; ox; rōse; ô in bought; coin; boŏk; toō; form; out; up; ūse; tûrn; ə sound in about, chicken, pencil, cannon, circus; chair; hw in which; ring; shop; thin; there; zh in treasure.

setting (set´ ting) *v.* A form of the verb **set:** To go down below the horizon.

settlers (set´ tlûrz) *n.* Plural form of **settler:** A person who makes a new home in a new land or country.

shared (shārd) *v.* Past tense of **share:** To use with another or others.

shattered (shat´ tûrd) *adj.* Destroyed completely.

sheltered (shel´ tûrd) *adj.* Protected from danger.

shingle (shin´ gəl) *v.* To cover with shingles.

shock waves (shok´ wāvz) *n.* Plural form of **shock wave:** A vibration after a violent collision of tectonic plates.

sigh (sī) *n.* A long, deep breathing sound caused by sadness, tiredness, or relief.

signs (sīnz) *n.* Plural form of **sign:** A trace.

siren (sī´ rən) *n.* A device that makes a loud, shrill sound.

site (sīt) *n.* A location.

slightly (slīt´ lē) *adv.* Just a little.

sliver (sliv´ ûr) *n.* A thin, narrow piece.

sliver

sneak (snēk) *v.* To go quietly without being seen.

soaked (sōkd) *v.* A form of the verb **soak:** To take in; to absorb.

soared (sord) *v.* Past tense of **soar:** To fly.

solar system (sō´ lûr sis´ təm) *n.* The sun and all the planets, satellites, asteroids, and comets that revolve around it.

squinty (skwint´ ē) *adj.* Eyes partly closed.

stark (stärk) *adj.* Lonely; empty.

stored (stord) *v.* Past tense of **store:** To put away for future use.

stormed (stormd) *v.* Past tense of **storm:** To rush in with boldness and force.

streaming (strēm´ ing) *adj.* Running; flowing.

stroked (strōkd) *v.* Past tense of **stroke:** To rub gently.

struggled (stru´ gəld) *v.* Past tense of **struggle:** To make a great effort.

stump (stump) *n.* Part of tree left over after cutting away at the trunk.

stump

sturdy (stûr´ dē) *adj.* Strong; hardy.

surplus (sûr´ plus) *n.* An amount greater than what is needed.

survived (sûr vīvd´) *v.* Past tense of **survive:** To stay alive.

tectonic plates (tek tôn´ik plāts) *n.* Plural form of **tectonic plate:** A large piece of rock under the earth's surface.

telescopes (tel´ ə scōps) *n.* Plural form of **telescope:** An instrument that makes distant objects seem larger and nearer.

tepees (tē´ pēz) *n.* Plural form of **tepee:** A portable house used by Native Americans.

thrilling (thril´ ing) *adj.* Exciting.

tide (tīd) *n.* The rise and fall of the sea.

tight (tīt) *adj.* Fitting very closely together.

tilted (tilt´ əd) *adj.* On a slant.

timid (tim´ id) *adj.* Easily frightened; lacking boldness.

Pronunciation Key: at; lāte; câre; fäther; set; mē; it; kīte; ox; rōse; ô in bought; coin; boŏk; toō; form; out; up; ūse; tûrn; ə sound in about, chicken, pencil, cannon, circus; chair; hw in which; ring; shop; thin; there; zh in treasure.

top (top) *n.* A spinning toy.

top

toppled (top´ pəld) *v.* Past tense of **topple:** To fall or make fall forward.

tough (tuf) *adj.* Hard to deal with or do; demanding.

traditions (trəd ish´ ənz) *n.* Plural form of **tradition:** The practice of passing down customs, beliefs, or other knowledge from parents to their children.

transform (trans form´) *v.* To change the form or condition of something.

treasured (trezh´ ûrd) *adj.* Valued highly.

treasures (trezh´ ûrz) *n.* Plural form of **treasure:** Something special; a keepsake.

trembled (trem´ bəld) *v.* Past tense of **tremble:** To shake.

trickle (trik´ əl) *n.* A small amount.

universe (ū´ ni vûrs) *n.* Everything that exists in our solar system and all of space.

vegetation (vej´ ə tā´ shən) *n.* Plant life.

voyage (voi´ əj) *v.* To journey by water or through space.

voyage

waded (wād´ əd) *v.* Past tense of **wade:** To walk through water.

waning (wān´ ing) *adj.* Becoming smaller.

waxing (waks´ ing) *adj.* Becoming bigger.

works (wûrks) *v.* A form of the verb **work:** To shape, as by pressing or rolling.

Photo Credits